Thinking Through the Bible
S·E·R·I·E·S

Thinking Through

John's
Epistles

L. A. Mott, Jr.

Jacksonville, Florida

Published by **Sunesis Publishing Company**
11908 Gran Meadows Way, Jacksonville, FL 32258
www.sunesispublishing.com

The Apostle Paul desired that disciples would receive "all riches of the full assurance of understanding, that they may know the mystery of God, even Christ, in whom are all the treasures of wisdom and knowledge hidden" (Colossians 2:1–3, ASV). The Greek word translated "understanding" is *sunesis*, and the mission of *Sunesis Publishing* is to provide resources which will assist disciples in their quest for these riches.

Publisher's Cataloging-in-Publication

Mott, L. A.
  Thinking through John's Epistles/ L.A. Mott, Jr. —
1st ed.
  p. cm. — (Thinking through the Bible series)
  LCCN: 2004097262
  ISBN: 0971648727

  1. Bible. N.T. Epistles of John—Commentaries. I. Title.

BS2805.53.M75 2004   227'.9407

Printed in Canada

This little book is inscribed

with pride and affection ...

To My Daughter,

Deborah Jo Cale

Maybe the best teacher of us all

Also by L. A. Mott, Jr.

Thinking Through John's Epistles: Study Questions
Thinking Through John's Epistles **on Cassette**
lecture series which complements the book

Thinking Through the Bible Series
Wisdom and Poetry

Thinking Through John

Thinking Through Acts

Paul's Gospel Among the Gentiles
(on the epistle to the Romans)

Thinking Through Second Corinthians

Thinking Through Philippians

Hebrews & James

Thinking Through Revelation

Also Available
a series of study guides on the entire Bible
and accompanying cassette tapes of the author's classes

See page 125 for complete list and order form.

Table of Contents

Abbreviations

AG:	Arndt & Gingrich, *Greek-English Lexicon*
ASV:	*American Standard Version of the Bible*
EDNT:	*Exegetical Dictionary of the New Testament*
EGT:	*Expositor's Greek Testament*
Grk:	Greek
GT:	Grimm-Thayer, *Greek-English Lexicon*
KJV:	*King James Version of the Bible*
NEB:	*New English Bible*
NASB:	*New American Standard Bible*
NIV:	*New International Version*
NKJ:	*New King James Version*
NT:	New Testament
OT:	Old Testament
RSV:	*Revised Standard Version*
TDNT:	*Theological Dictionary of the New Testament*
Trench:	R. C. Trench, *Synonyms of the New Testament*
VED:	W. E. Vine, *Expository Dictionary of the New Testament*

Preface

Two applications give particular modern relevance to the epistles of John. Modernists hold that Christianity must be reinterpreted and redefined in the light of new knowledge in every age. But the apostle John, one of the original witnesses of the Christ, chosen by Jesus Christ to speak for him, has anticipated such views. False teachers had risen, claiming to have new and more enlightened understanding of Christianity. John tells his readers that they must go back to the beginning, back to the original witnesses of Christ Jesus, and to examine and test the new teaching in the light of their testimony. Any teaching must stand or fall on the basis of whether it agrees with the testimony of the original witnesses. Christianity is defined by Jesus' chosen witnesses. Any teaching that does not agree with their testimony is not Christianity. One may not like Christianity. He may not believe it is true. But the testimony of the apostles defines what it is. Whatever one may call a new religion that does not submit to the authority of these witnesses, it is not Christianity. A rose by any other name may smell just as sweet. But calling your overflowing septic tank a rose will not make it a rose. Nor will it smell like a rose.

John has drawn the lines between light and darkness, truth and error, Christianity and Antichristianity, children of God and children of the devil; and he has make the lines so clear that no one need be deceived. The lines are drawn with the authority of an apostle and a witness of Christ. We must study these epistles to learn where the lines are drawn. In the following exposition I have not critiqued the places where modern believers draw lines of fellowship. But I have tried very hard to understand and to explain where the apostle John drew them. We must learn to draw the lines where the apostles drew them.

I have learned from experts on the original language such as A. E. Brooke, B. F. Westcott and Raymond E. Brown. R. C. H. Lenski is always worth reading. So also I. Howard Marshall.

With this publication, my *Thinking Through ...* series now includes all the writings of John, and I want to publish an idea I have had for quite a while now, namely, that all the writings of John be studied one after the other. What a power packed year of study that could be!

I have written study questions on these epistles, but have not included them in this volume in order to keep the price down for those who may want the exposition without the questions. The questions are available in a companion volume for those who wish to use them in a class.

First John: A Modern Book

Sometime in the early nineties I had the opportunity to speak to the youth group of a Congregational Church presided over by a modernist preacher. One couple had stumbled into this church from a more traditional background, and somehow had become leaders of the youth group. At length, spiritually starved by the chaff being served up by the preacher, they asked for a Bible study. This preacher's idea of how to comply with that request was to conduct a class based on a book from one Bishop Spong entitled *Rescuing the Bible from the Fundamentalists*. I was given a copy, and read it. Not far into it I began to realize that I had read this stuff before. Bishop Spong was parroting the infidel Thomas Paine's line in *The Age of Reason*, which I had read in my youth. Like Paine before him, he was attacking the Bible from one end to the other. I have no idea how such a man came to be a bishop in the Episcopal Church, but I do know one thing. The bishop, whose job was to protect the sheep from the wolves (cf. Acts 20:28–30), was actually one of the wolves. One of the references footnoted by him was Sigmund Freud's *Moses and Monotheism*. At one place the bishop raised the question how we knew that our God was any better than the gods worshipped in other religions.

My purpose is not to review the entire book, but to call attention to one modernistic position taken by the bishop. He contended that Christianity must be reinterpreted in every age and adapted to the thinking and new understanding of the age. Neither the bishop nor the modernistic Congregational preacher encountered by me seemed to be aware that the New Testament contains one book which anticipates such teachers as they. That book is the first epistle of John. But unfortunately for these two men, this apostolic spokesman for Christ took quite a different line about Christianity. He anticipates the coming of teachers who would claim new, progressive knowledge (2:18–27). But instead of taking the view that Christianity must be adapted to these new insights, he tells the Christians under his influence that they must hold on to the teaching which they received at the beginning (2:24, 27); that all such new teaching must be judged in the light of the testimony of the original apostolic witnesses (4:1–6). It would either stand or fall, depending on whether it agreed with the original witnesses. Anyone who would not listen to these original spokesmen for Christ was not of God. Thus John equips Christians to deal with such teachers by taking them back to the beginning and to the testimony of the original witnesses of Jesus Christ. He draws the lines of fellowship against such antichrists as Bishop Spong. The line is drawn between light and darkness (1:5–7); between obedience and disobedience (2:3–6); between truth and the liar (2:18–27); between the children of God and the children of the devil (2:28–ch. 3); between the Spirit of truth and the spirit of error (4:1–6). A ring of certainty is heard throughout the epistle and is finally sounded forth most emphatically at the end. Three times at the end the apostle will say: "We know!" (5:18–21).

Thus there is no need for disciples of Jesus to be confused by new and different teaching. The lines are clearly drawn, and they are drawn by one with the authority of an apostle and an eyewitness of Christ Jesus. We need not be in doubt. We can know the truth.

I will not spend much time discussing the authorship of the epistles ascribed to John, but instead, dive right into the text. I made an argument in *Thinking Through John* (notes on John 21) supporting the position that the Gospel of John was written by the apostle John. That the epistles come from the same author can be argued on the ground of the close relationship between the epistles and the Gospel. This point can best be appreciated if the Epistles of John are studied right on the heels of the Gospel, and that is my recommendation.

FIRST JOHN 1:1–4
Prologue: The Subject Matter of First John

John begins by setting forth his subject, that which he and his colleagues declare and which is now put into writing. The prologue also indicates the authority by which he writes and the certainty of what he declares. It is the authority of a witness to the Christ.

The Thing Declared by Witnesses (3) Concerning the Word of Life (1)

The subject on which John writes is that which was declared by the witnesses (v. 3) concerning the word of life (v. 1). Pay close attention to the description. This message deals with:

1. That which was from the beginning. But what is meant by *the beginning*? The epistle speaks of the beginning in two senses. Sometimes reference is made to the absolute beginning (2:13f; 3:8). Some, therefore, think of the absolute beginning, as in the prologue to John (1:1). But the word is also used for the beginning in a relative sense, for what the readers had first learned from apostolic teachers: the "old commandment which you had from the beginning" (2:7); "that which you heard from the beginning" (2:24); "the message which you heard from the beginning" (3:11). See also Second John 5–6.

Which sense applies here? Two points make the second sense more probable. One is the other parallel clauses which describe the same thing. *That which was from the beginning* is also *that which we have heard, that which we have seen ... etc.* This parallelism seems to identify the beginning with the revelation made through Christ.

Then further, all of these clauses are connected with *concerning the word of life.* So, as that which we have heard, seen, beheld, and our hands handled concerned the word of life, so also that which is from the beginning was about the word of life. That connection also points to a relative rather than an absolute beginning, namely the beginning of the revelation through Christ.

So, with false teachers appearing among the Christians, setting forth new views of Christ, John takes his readers back to the beginning for the understanding of the truth. This new teaching is not true and never has been true, not from the beginning. "From the beginning it has not been so," as Jesus said about another matter (Matt. 19:8).

The remaining clauses all speak to the authority and certainty of that which was from the beginning:

2. That which we have heard ... but not just heard:

3. That which we have seen with our eyes ... our very own eyes ... but again, not just seen, but more:

4. That which we beheld. The Greek *theomai* is more than just seeing; it is to gaze upon with interest, almost perhaps: make a study of. But even that does not exhaust the experience of the witnesses, for John has one more clause to add:

5. ... and our hands handled. John is certainly referring to the post-resurrection experience of the once dead, but now alive Christ which is reported in Luke 24:39–40 and John 20:20, 25 & 27.

All five of these clauses are connected with the phrase ...

Concerning the Word of Life (1)

But should *Word* be capitalized (some versions), as having a personal reference, according to the usage in John 1:1, 14? Or does it mean *the message of life*, in which case the expression would have a parallel in Philippians 2:16?[1] Probably the latter is correct. In any case, the emphasis is on *life* (as manifested in the person Jesus Christ) rather than on *word*, and this will be the point which is elaborated and expounded upon in verse 2.

Life Elaborated and Expounded (2)

1. John is plainly referring to the life manifested in Christ Jesus, which is given such emphasis in his Gospel:

"In him was life; and the life was the light of men" (John 1:4).

"... even so must the Son of man be lifted up; that whosoever believes may in him have eternal life" (John 3:14–15).

"For God so loved the world, that he gave his only begotten Son, that whosoever believes on him should not perish, but have eternal life" (John 3:16).

---

[1] Cf. Acts 5:20 which speaks of *all the words of this life.*

"He that believes on the Son has eternal life; ..." (John 3:36).

"For as the Father raises the dead and gives them life, even so the Son also gives life to whom he will" (John 5:21).

"Verily, verily, I say unto you, He that hears my word, and believes him that sent me, has eternal life, and comes not into judgment, but has passed out of death into life. Verily, verily, I say unto you, The hour comes, and now is, when the dead shall hear the voice of the Son of God; and they that hear shall live. For as the Father has life in himself, even so gave he to the Son also to have life in himself: ..." (John 5:24–26).

The Gospel has many other such passages, of course, but notice the following particularly:

Jesus claims, "... the words that I have spoken unto you are spirit, and are life" (John 6:63b), and Peter was certainly listening, for when Jesus inquires whether the twelve may wish to abandon him as had the great mass of the crowd, "Simon Peter answered him, Lord, to whom shall we go? You have the words of eternal life" (John 6:68).

Finally, the claim of Jesus: "I am the way, and the truth, and the life" (John 14:6).

2. Then notice that *the author includes himself among those who are witnesses to the life in Christ*: "and we have seen, and bear witness, and declare unto you the life."

3. *This life is then further defined* as "the eternal life (cf. John 6:40, 47–51, 58, 68; 8:51; 11:25–26), which was with the Father, and was manifested unto us."

Plainly, John is referring to the manifestation of eternal life in Christ Jesus. It would not be an overstatement to call verses 1 & 2 a summary of the Gospel of John.

The Sentence Structure (of Verse 1) Resumed (in 3)

Observe four points on verse 3:

1. *That which we have seen and heard* summarizes verse 1.

2. That very thing, says the author, the experience of which was treated more fully in verse 1 and is now briefly summarized, is what *we declare to you also*.

3. The *purpose* for which John and his colleagues declare that which they have experienced as witnesses to such as the readers is then stated: "that you also may have fellowship with us." The Greek *koinonia* (fellowship) is a partnership, a joint participation, a sharing in common. Thus the witnesses declare that which they have experienced to those who are not witnesses, so that the latter may share in the life which had been manifested to the witnesses.

4. The fellowship of the apostolic witnesses, into which the readers and other non-witnesses like them have been brought by the declaration of the witnesses, is then said to be nothing less than *a fellowship with the Father, and with his Son Jesus Christ.*

Thus the readers are introduced into fellowship with God by being brought into fellowship with the witnesses. Fellowship with the apostles is the means by which people are brought into fellowship with God. Many people think they can have fellowship with God while rejecting the apostolic testimony. (That is the view of Bishop Spong referred to in the preface, for example.) But the testimony of the apostles is the means by which people are brought into fellowship with the apostles, which is a fellowship with the Father and Son. There is simply no fellowship with God without fellowship with the apostolic witnesses.

The Testimony Put in Writing (4)

1. *And these things we write*, says John, referring to the things of which he has previously spoken: the things manifested, seen, heard and declared. Thus the things that made it possible for people to be brought into fellowship with the apostles, and hence to share in their fellowship with God, the Father and the Son, have now been put into writing; so that it is possible for people throughout the ages to have fellowship with God through the writings of the witnesses preserved in the New Testament documents. Praise the Lord! What a precious treasure is found in these ancient writings!

2. *The purpose for writing these things* is then stated: "that our joy may be made full." It is the joy of a mission successfully accomplished.

Summary of the Message Heard and Announced, and Its Bearing on Fellowship with God

Summary of the Message Heard From Christ and Announced by the Witnesses (5)

The message heard from Christ Jesus and now announced to the readers is summarized in an assertion about God: *God is light.* Now the imagery of light and darkness is characteristic of John's writing. It makes sense to draw upon John's other references to this imagery for help in the interpretation of the present passage. If we follow that common sense approach, we will not go astray in our understanding of this assertion about God or of what is meant by walking in the light in verse 7. We shall begin with this epistle:

First John 2:7–11. The light shines (8b). It illuminates. To be in the light is to have one's pathway illuminated, so that "there is no occasion of stumbling in him" (10). On the other hand, to walk "in the darkness" means there is no light to illuminate the way, so that a person cannot see where he is going (11).

Now we turn to the Gospel:

John 1:4–9. Again, the light shines (5); it illuminates (9).

John 3:19–21. The light exposes and reproves or convicts (20); it makes one's works manifest (21).

John 8:12. Jesus claims to be "the light of the world"; the effect is: "he that follows me shall not walk in the darkness, but shall have the light of life." Compare 1:4 for "the light of life."

John 9:4–5. Day is the time to work; "the night comes, when no man can work." He cannot see to work in the darkness of night. "When I am in the world, I am the light of the world." After making this claim Jesus establishes it by giving sight to "a man blind from his birth," who had never seen the light of day. To be blind is to be in darkness; to be able to see is to be in the light. The chapter closes with an application of the imagery to Pharisees as spiritually blinded by the coming of the light (vv. 39–41), a concept explained by 3:19–21. They loved the darkness rather than the light, since the light exposed their evil works, and therefore did not come to the light, but retreated to the darkness.

John 11:9–10. In the daytime one does not stumble "because he sees the light of this world. But if one walks in the night, he stumbles, because the light is not in him." He cannot see where he is going in the darkness of night, and is therefore liable to stumble against some unseen obstacle in his way. The application in context is that Jesus need not fear death as long as it is day. But again the point of the imagery is that light illuminates. One can see where he is going in the light of day, but cannot see at night, and so may stumble.

John 12:35–36. In response to a question, Jesus challenges the Jews to make good use of the light while they have it. The illumination received from the light (himself) will provide the answer to all questions. But they must not wait to be overtaken by the darkness; "he that walks in the darkness does not know where he is going." But if they will make proper use of the light while they have it they can "become sons of light."

John 12:46. "I am come a light into the world, that whosoever believes on me may not abide in the darkness."

So over and over again, the same point is made. Light illuminates; it enables one to see. But to be in darkness is not to know; not to see; and so, to be liable to stumble over something.

God is light. He is characterized by absolute knowledge and truth. As John adds, not the least speck of darkness is to be found in him. The darkness of ignorance and error that is so characteristic of the world in general is not found in him at all. That is what the apostles learned about God from Jesus, who had true knowledge and spoke absolutely nothing but truth and reality.

Bearing of This Message on Fellowship With God and With One Another (6–7)

The nature of God determines the condition of fellowship with God and with all others in fellowship with him. Since God is light, only light, and has no darkness at all in him, then we cannot claim fellowship with him while walking in the darkness. Fellowship is joint participation or sharing in common. But God has no darkness in which one may participate or share. So the claim to have fellowship with God while walking in darkness is false, and the persons making it are simply not dealing in reality. They do not practice the truth. Only "if we walk in the light" of the revelation of God made through Christ can we have fellowship with God.

"But if we walk in the light, as he is in the light," not only do we have fellowship with God, but two additional consequences follow:

1. "We have fellowship one with another" (contrast 2:19)—a joint participation or sharing in common with all others who participate or share in the light.

2. "The blood of Jesus his Son cleanses us from all sin." Sin is the great hindrance to fellowship with God. But as long as we walk in the light of the revelation of God in Christ, all sin is wiped out.

When the consequences of walking in the light are enumerated, we see that this metaphor cannot mean to walk in sinless perfection; otherwise one would have no sin to be cleansed by the blood of Jesus. So we must insist on interpreting "the light" from the use John has elsewhere made of this imagery. (See passages and discussion above.) The metaphor refers to the light of the revelation of God in Christ.

The condition of continued fellowship with God is not sinless perfection, but remaining in the light of divine revelation; continuing in that relationship which makes forgiveness possible.

Another False Position Exposed: The Denial of Sin (8–10)

When we walk in the light of divine revelation, the light makes manifest the nature of our works (cf. John 3:21). It exposes our sins.

Now we may react in one of two ways. One is to deny our sins, to "say that we have no sin." That is the way many reacted to the coming of the light into the world. They hated the light because it exposed their evil works. So they did not come to the light because they did not want their works to be exposed (John 3:19–21).

So it is if Christians deny their sin. The denial represents a retreat to the darkness of self-deception. "If we say that we have no sin, we deceive ourselves,[2] and the truth is not in us." We deny the thing that

---

[2] Greek *planao*: *"to cause to stray, to lead astray, lead aside from the right way,"* literally of men wandering in the deserts, mountains and caves (Heb. 11:38), of sheep who go astray (Matt. 18:12–13) and of men who go astray as sheep do ["of men who had strayed from the right way" (AG) (1 Pet. 2:25); "metaphorically to lead away from the truth, *to lead into error, to deceive*" (GT, 514; cf. AG, 665).

is true, and so the truth has no home in us. We live under an illusion, a denial of reality. Thus we retreat back into the darkness.

Now the alternative follows: The right way to deal with the sins in our lives. The presence of sin in a Christian's life need not destroy fellowship with God. But we must deal with the sins exposed by the light in the right way, which is simply to acknowledge our sins and to seek forgiveness from God. "If we confess our sins, he is faithful and righteous to forgive us our sins, and to cleanse us from all unrighteousness."

The consequences of the denial of sin are put even stronger in verse 10. "If we say that we have not sinned,"[3] two consequences follow:

1. *We make God a liar*, for he says we have sinned (cf. Rom. 3:9–18), just as one who does not believe the testimony God has borne concerning his Son is making God a liar (1 John 5:10).

2. *"His word is not in us."* God's word assumes the sinfulness of mankind from beginning to end. The one who accepts the witness God has borne concerning his Son and "believes on the Son of God has the witness in him" (1 John 5:9–10). Of course the one who does not believe rejects that testimony and does not have that testimony within him. So also one who rejects God's testimony concerning the sinfulness of mankind does not have God's word in him.

John's Purpose (2:1a)

"These things write I unto you that you may not sin." Nothing John has asserted about the universality of sin should cause one to conclude that sin is inevitable and so to be lenient in his judgments on sin. Nor should the assurances of the possibility of forgiveness lead one to take sin lightly. The writer recognizes the universality of sin, but does not wish to encourage sin. To the contrary, he wishes his "little children" to take sin seriously, and writes to try to prevent them from sinning.[4]

---

[3] Perfect tense, referring to something done in the past, the effect of which continues in the present; therefore, "we have not sinned" in the past, so that we now "have sin" in the present (cf. v. 8).

[4] We should also bear the writer's purpose in mind when we come to 3:6, 9. The writer's purpose is not to assure his readers of the impossibility of sin, but rather, to try to discourage them from sinning or taking sin lightly.

Provision Established in Case of Sin (2:1b–2)

We feel, I think, that 1b should begin with *But*, but it begins with *And*, the statements describing the provision God has made in the event that one sins simply being added on to the previous statement. No contrast with 1a is intended. John writes in order that his readers may not sin, and in the event they do, he assures them of the provision God has made to deal with sin.

1. *"We have an Advocate with the Father" (1b).* The Greek *parakletos* was originally one called to someone's aid. The technical meaning "advocate, lawyer, attorney" is actually rare. The few occurrences in pre-Christian and extra-Christian literature "have for the most part a more general meaning: one who appears in another's behalf, mediator, intercessor, helper" (AG, 618).

The term designates Jesus Christ as our intercessor (1 John 2:1). The application of this term to Jesus was also implied, though perhaps in another sense, by calling the Holy Spirit "another paraclete" (John 14:16). It is applied to the Holy Spirit in the general sense of "helper" (John 14:16, 26; 15:26; 16:7), the nature of the help provided being explained in the context.[5]

The present occurrence of the term is defined: "one who pleads another's cause with one, an intercessor ... so of Christ, in his exaltation at God's right hand, pleading with God the Father for the pardon of our sins" (GT, 483).

"The accuser of our brothers is cast down, who accuseth them before our God day and night" (Rev. 12:10). The one who pleads against us has lost his place in court (Job 1:6–2:7; Zech. 3:1–3; Rev. 12:7–12, esp. 10b), and "believers now have someone who defends them before God instead of accusing them" (Brown).

Our Advocate with the Father is *Jesus Christ the righteous.* "In him is no sin" (3:5b). Having no sin of his own for which he must

---

[5] The help implied in the word *parakletos* is clearly administered by means of words. So in the case of the Holy Spirit, who teaches, brings to remembrance, bears witness and guides into the truth. So also in the implied reference of this term to Jesus. So, finally, in the case of our *parakletos* with or toward (Grk *pros*) the Father. The difference here is that the words are directed to the Father rather than to human beings. It is therefore a matter of intercession on our behalf.

answer, he pleads the case for us. "The supplication of a righteous man avails much in its working" (James 5:16).

2. *"And he is the propitiation for our sins" (2a)*, which explains the ground of the intercessor's plea. He does not plead our case on the ground of our innocence, but on the ground of his being the *hilasmos* for our sins. But what is meant by that? Does the word mean propitiation, expiation, or does it contain an element of each?

The Greek *hilasmos* appears in the New Testament only in First John, here and in 4:10. In pagan usage, it has the sense of propitiation, with the idea of appeasing or placating an offended and angry deity. The wrath of God is in fact a Biblical concept (Micah 7:18; John 3:36; Rom. 1:18). It is the attitude of a holy God against the sin and rebellion of mankind; it is wrath which must be turned away by sacrifice for sin.

But God delights in mercy and wants to forgive. He himself takes the initiative to provide the means: the expiatory or atoning sacrifice by which sin is covered (1 John 4:10).

The day of atonement in the Greek Old Testament is the day *tou hilasmou* (at Lev. 25:9). Atonement is effected by means of blood (Lev. 17:11), which lies near in the context: "the blood of Jesus his Son cleanses us from all sin" (1 John 1:7).

Therefore, our Advocate speaks for us not on the ground of what we have done, but on the ground of what he has done: the expiatory sacrifice by which he made forgiveness possible.

Jesus is not only "the propitiation for our sins," but in fact the propitiation "for the whole world" (2b). He died even for those who will eventually be lost (Rom. 14:15; 2 Pet. 2:1). But Jesus is not said to be "an Advocate" for the whole world. How can we know that we are in the right relationship with God, so that "the blood of Jesus his Son" is actually applied for us by the intercession of Christ Jesus? This matter of the right relationship is discussed in the following passage.

Fellowship with God has been shown to depend upon joint participation with him in the light, referring to God's revelation of himself in Christ. Walking in the light does not imply sinlessness. But John does not want anything he has written to be understood as encouraging sin or a casual attitude toward sin. However, in the event that one in fellowship with God falls into sin, provision has been made to deal with sin, so that fellowship with God may continue. That provision involves the intercession of Jesus Christ with the Father on our behalf, which is grounded on his own propitiatory sacrifice for our sins. He is also the propitiation "for the whole world." But not everyone in the whole world can claim to have Jesus Christ as "an Advocate with the Father." The application of the propitiation depends on persons being in the right relationship with the Intercessor. So how can we know that we "know him" as our "Advocate with the Father"? That would seem to be the point to which we arrive at First John 2:3.

KEEPING HIS COMMANDMENTS THE TEST OF THE RELATIONSHIP
FIRST JOHN 2:3–6

"Hereby We Know" (3)

The point is simply added to what precedes by means of "And," which seems to justify the connection I have made with the preceding verses: "And in this we know that we know him, if we keep his commandments." The second *know* is a perfect tense, implying having come to know him in the past, with this knowledge continuing to have its effect in the present. It is not merely a mental or academic knowledge that John has in mind, but refers to an intimate relationship with him. Thus the expressions "in him" (5b) and to abide "in him" (6) will be used interchangeably with knowing him. So, as I have argued above, John is talking about having the kind of relationship with Christ that makes him our "Advocate with the Father."

Previously John has dealt with the claim to have fellowship with God the Father (1:6). But here the whole context seems to require a reference to the relationship with Christ our Advocate. *Him* must be understood both in the light of the immediate context, which would include the preceding verses (1–2) as well as the following verses. With regard to the latter, consider especially that the repeated references to "him" ends with a reference to walking "as he walked"—certainly a reference to the conduct of the incarnate Christ; and further, that "his commandments" (4) are at length summarized in terms of the "new commandment" given by Christ Jesus (7–11 with John 13:34–35).

John anticipates the claim to have a relationship with deity that has no effect on behavior. But the test of the relationship is the keeping of his commandments. We are assured that "we know him, if we keep his commandments."

False Claim Exposed and the True Test Declared (4–5)

John anticipates that someone may claim to know the Christ while not keeping his commandments: "He that says, I know him, and does not keep his commandments, is a liar, and the truth is not in him" (4). The claim is to a knowledge of deity that does not affect behavior. It is a false claim. The man who so claims is a liar. It is not merely that he is self-deceived (cf. 1:8). He claims that which does not conform to reality and does not have the truth in him.

The exposure of the false claim is followed by the truth about one in Christ (5). It is not the one who merely claims to know Christ, "but whoever keeps his word"[6] that is in the right relationship with Christ. "Truly in that one the love of God has been perfected." The Greek adverb *alethos* is defined: "truly, in truth, really, actually" (AG, 37). In contrast to that one who claims to know him, but does not keep his commandments, in whom the truth (*aletheia*) does not exist, it is actually, truly, or really "whoever keeps his word" that is in Christ. It is that one in whom "the love of God has been perfected."[7]

---

[6] *His word* may include more than commandments and refer to the entirety of his message. But keeping his word is interchangeable with keeping his commandments. So this distinction may not be significant here.

[7] Consider the other occurrences of the adverb *alethos* in the writings of John. It is used of a genuine Israelite, one truly an Israelite (John 1:47); "truly the

note continued on next page

The Greek verb *teleioo* means to bring to an end or goal (*telos*). *The love of God has been brought to its end in him.* Two points will help with the interpretation.

First, consider the way "his commandments" and "his word" are soon to be summarized in Jesus' commandment to "love one another" (7–11 with John 13:34–35). John's thought in the keeping of his commandments has primary reference to the various commandments that give direction about loving each other.

Second, consider how the thought of this verse is elaborated in this epistle. The love of Christ was manifested at the cross and his desire is that that same love be in us (3:16). But "how does the love of God abide in" one who closes his heart to a needy brother? (3:17). Then consider 4:12 in its context, beginning at verse 7. "If we love one another, God abides in us, and his love is perfected in us." So the love of God that was manifested in the gift of his Son (9–10) reaches its end in us when we love each other with that same sacrificial love.

Finally, to summarize, keeping his word means loving our brothers, and when we love our brothers the love of God manifested at the cross has reached its end in us.

Finally John rounds out the discussion beginning at verse 3 by repeating the point with which he started: "In this we know that we are in him" (5b). *In this* is explained by what has just been said as referring to the keeping of his commandments or the keeping of his word. That is the assurance we have "that we are in him." But the discussion started with the assurance we have "that we know him." The change of terminology (5b) proves what has been said above about the meaning of "know him," as referring to an intimate relationship with him.

Obligation of One Who Claims to Remain in Christ (6)

John has shown how we may be sure "that we are in Christ," and now closes the development of thought by asserting the obligation of one who claims to be in Christ: "He who says he remains in him ought

---

Savior of the world" (John 4:42)—no doubt about it!; "truly the prophet that comes into the world" (John 6:14); real meat and drink in contrast to that which only simulates reality (John 6:55, Received Text); what someone knows truly (John 7:26); truly the prophet (7:40); "truly my disciples" (John 8:31); "they knew truly that I came forth from you" (John 17:8).

himself also to walk even as he walked." John 13:34–35 (with 1 John 2:7–11) was used to explain the keeping of the commandments. Now we can make use of the Gospel once more to explain walking as Christ walked. The new commandment given by Christ was "that you love one another; even as I have loved you, that you also love one another." Jesus goes on to say that this sacrificial love for each other was the way men would be able to recognize them as disciples. First John 2:6 is certainly consistent with Jesus' thought when John says the one who claims to be in Christ is obligated to walk as he walked—keeping his commandments, loving his brothers, just as Jesus had. If he does not, his claim to know Christ or to "remain in him" is falsified. He is, plain and simple, "a liar, and the truth is not in him."

THE COMMANDMENT BOTH OLD AND NEW
FIRST JOHN 2:7–11

John writes about a commandment that is old (7), and yet new (8). It is old in one sense, but new in another. The commandment he has in mind most likely has reference to the obligation expressed by the word "ought" in verse 6, the obligation to walk as Jesus walked. As we shall soon see (9–11), the commandment John has in mind is the command to love one's brother. It is a single commandment which embodies all "his commandments" (4) about the way the brothers should relate to each other. This explanation of the commandment (7–8) is also confirmed by the apparent allusion to the new commandment Jesus gave "that you love one another; even as I have loved you, that you also love one another" (John 13:34). This explanation of his commandment, "that you love one another, even as I have loved you" is then repeated (in John 15:12), in a passage where "commandment" and "commandments" are interchanged (John 15:10 with 12), as they are in the present text.

Not a New Commandment (7)

"New" is defined in verse 7 in terms of age. The commandment of which John speaks is not of recent origin; it is not innovative. It is not a new commandment, "but an old commandment which you had from the beginning: the old commandment is the word which you heard." *From the beginning* would seem to refer to the time when the gospel was first introduced to them. The commandment which they heard at that time went all the way back to Jesus. It was not something new.

Yet a New Commandment (8)

When John now calls the commandment he writes to them "a new commandment" he does not mean it is recent. As he will explain, he is referring to the vitality of the commandment. It continues to be true and valid. "Old" sometimes refers to that which is obsolete, outdated, and no longer true. Thus when God spoke in Jeremiah 31:31–34 of a new covenant, he implied that the first covenant was old (Heb. 8:13a). "But that which is becoming old and aged is nigh unto vanishing away" (Heb. 8:13b). That was already true of the first covenant in the time of Jeremiah, some 600 years before Christ. The same thing is true of the material universe: It gets old and vanishes away. That is true of the creation, but it is not true of the Creator, who remains the same and his years unfailing (Heb. 1:10–12).

The new commandment of which John speaks is not new in the sense of being of recent date; it is old (7). But it is not old in the sense of becoming obsolete, no longer true and valid, and therefore ready to pass away. When one thinks in those terms, it will always be "a new commandment." It will never be obsolete and outdated.

That is the explanation John makes of the newness of the new commandment: "which thing is true in him and in you." In this sense, the commandment will always be new; it will never be outdated.

The neuter *which thing* creates a difficulty, since it does not agree with the Greek feminine noun for *commandment*. But perhaps the antecedent is not commandment, but the whole preceding clause, i. e. "the principal sentence as a whole, the fact that the old commandment is, notwithstanding, *new*" (Findlay).

The truth of the newness of the commandment is being realized *in him and in you,* which agrees with the probability suggested above that the commandment refers to the obligation *to walk as he walked* (6), this obligation, in turn, alluding to the new commandment Jesus gave to love one another as he had loved them (John 13:34; 15:12). Jesus had manifested a new kind of love, so different from the darkness of the world, when he laid down his life for others (cf. 2:2; 3:16), which love continues to be manifested in his present intercession (2:1b); and that love is also manifested in his disciples when they walk as he walked.

An explanation of the truth of this manifestation of newness follows: "because the darkness is passing away, and the true light already shines" (8b). It is not the light that is passing away as being old, worn out and obsolete, but the darkness of the old way of life. Recall the explanation of light and darkness from the discussion of 1:5–7. *The darkness* refers to the ignorance and error of the world and the old way of life, the darkness that covered over the evil works of men (cf. John 3:19–21). Jesus had come into the world as *the true light* that provides light for the dark world (cf. esp. John 1:4–9, but also the whole list of passages given in the discussion of 1:5–7). That "true light" began to shine in the darkness and to illuminate the world with the coming of the Christ (John 1:4–9). It continues to shine as his disciples walk as he walked and manifest his word in the world (2:4–6). Already the darkness of ignorance and error was passing away, being banished by the shining of the true light. True, some would choose to remain in darkness (9), but the true light was shining, and it was possible for anyone who so chose to walk in the light. Those who remained in darkness would be without excuse.

Another False Claim Exposed (9)

One may claim to be "in the light," but if that claim is combined with hatred of his brother it is exposed as false. "He is in the darkness even until now." Even though "the true light already shines" (8b) this one remains in the darkness.

It seems likely that John already has in mind the false teachers soon to be expressly dealt with (2:18–27). They may claim to be progressive (cf. 2 John 9), to have new truth concerning God. But when they walked out of the apostolic fellowship they were exposed as not really belonging to the brotherhood in Christ (2:19). Their hatred and contempt for true brothers in Christ marked them as being "in the darkness," despite their claim to be "in the light."[8]

My brothers, take warning! Do you have superior light? Then share it and let it be tested in "the marketplace of ideas." But be careful how

---

[8] This argument is supported by Third John, where Gaius' support for teachers of the truth (2–8) is spoken of as a manifestation of love (6), and this in contrast to Diotrephes, who would not receive the brothers (9–10).

you treat your brothers in the heat of controversy. Something is surely wrong with your claim to be "in the light" if you hate your brothers. In fact your claim is exposed as false by your own behavior.

I cannot speak for others, but John works on my conscience at this point. Am I the only one who feels convicted by the truth of First John? I know I must not be. I have seen ugliness in others, those on the other side of many an issue. It has been easier to see it in them than in me. But I cannot be their accuser. The apostle must work conviction in other hearts. We can pray that we will understand John's message before it is too late. Meantime I probably ought to see myself as the only one with sin and even "darkness," as John would put it.

As I look back over a long "ministry" I know that I have often failed to love the brothers, and that over differences that were not near as weighty as the doctrinal issues dealt with in First John. If I were as bold as John I expect I would call my treatment of them by its right name. Some may think I am overstating the case. I never used the word "hate" with reference to the brothers. But the teachers John has specially in mind may not have used the word either; and the arrogance, self-righteousness and contempt that we manifest toward others are really expressions of hatred. We can be real clever at concealing ugly attitudes under cover of high-sounding, noble words.

The Difference Between Loving and Hating (10–11)

John expands upon his judgment on the false claim (9) by means of a contrast in the consequences for one who loves his brother and one who hates him. Whether we love or hate our brother is a critical point that really determines whether we are in the light or in the darkness. Furthermore, John adds consequences of being in the light and of being in the darkness, which provide understanding of what it means to be in the light and in the darkness.

First the consequences of loving one's brother: "He that loves his brother (1) remains in the light, and (2) there is no occasion of stumbling in him" (v. 10). Amazing! that love of one's brother can be singled out as giving evidence that one is in the light. But perhaps not so amazing when we consider that love of the brothers is the point to which God's love aims to bring us. The love of God, manifested by the gift of his Son (3:16–17; 4:8–10), attains its end or goal when we love each other (2:5; 4:12, 17–19), so that his love is manifested in us (3:17).

29

In that way love of the brothers gives evidence that we have been illuminated by the revelation of God in Christ and that we are living in that light. One may be on the right side of any number of issues without being in the light. But love of the brothers is the critical point at which we can know that we are in the light. It is that significant.

Having said that, though, I should point out that love is something John will find it necessary to define (3:16; 4:8–10). More than that, he will explain how we may "know that we love the children of God" (5:2; cf. 3:16–17). More is involved than a mere claim to love the brothers (3:18).

The further consequence of loving one's brother, and hence of being "in the light," is that "there is no occasion of stumbling in him." The contrast with the following verse (11) proves that of the two possible meanings of this line, John is thinking of our stumbling over something rather than giving occasion of stumbling to others, though that would doubtless be true as well. To be in the light means that our pathway is illuminated, we can see where we are going and need not stumble over some obstacle in the way.

Then the contrasting consequences when one hates his brother: "But he that hates his brother is in the darkness, and walks in the darkness, and does not know where he is going, because the darkness has blinded his eyes" (11).

The one who hates his brother is in the darkness and conducts himself in the darkness. His behavior does not manifest the least sign of any understanding of the divine purpose revealed in Christ Jesus. As far as he is concerned "the true light" might as well not have entered the world; might as well not be shining. He is still in the darkness, despite the illumination the true light has brought to the world.

The further consequence of being in the darkness indicates that we have been correct to understand the light as referring to the illumination of divine truth revealed through Christ. The one who hates his brother has not come to the light. He has made no use of the manifestation of God in Christ Jesus. The consequence is that he cannot see where he is going, "because the darkness has blinded his eyes." Therefore, he will surely lose his way or stumble over some obstacle in the path, which is unseen because it is hidden by the darkness that enshrouds him and prevents him from seeing.

FIRST JOHN 2:12–17
Warning Against Love of the World

A warning against love of the world (15–17), as will be defined below, is preceded by an assurance to the readers about their own spiritual position (12–14), which will lay a foundation for the warning. This warning against love of the world is probably also connected with the warning with regard to the false prophets that follows right on its heels (2:18–27). This connection is established by a later passage about these "false prophets" (4:1–6), in which John says concerning them: "They are out of[9] the world; on which account they speak out of[10] the world[11] and the world hears them" (4:5). Thus the warning against love of the world seems to build up to the warning about the false prophets whose message derives from the world rather than from God.

True Position (or Status) of the Readers, in Contrast to the False Claims of Opponents, as Ground for the Warning (12–14)

The exposure of claims with regard to one's relation to God must not be misunderstood. John is not making a judgment about the spiritual state of his readers. He assures them that they have met the tests by which one may be certain about his relationship with God. In contrast with those who make claims that are falsified by behavior, John was confident that what has been said previously about the true relationship with God does apply to his readers and he is able to communicate this assurance to them.

The assurances are given twice, and the commentators have struggled to understand why. The repetition pretty much simply repeats what was said the first time. Why? I have no explanation.

The first expression of these assurances uses the present tense: "I write unto you" three times (12–13b), clearly referring to John's present writing and in all likelihood includes the entire epistle.

The second is a past tense (Greek aorist): "I wrote unto you," and again, the commentators have struggled over the explanation. Of the

---

[9] The preposition *ek* indicating source.

[10] Again the Greek is ek.

[11] "*As* of the world," ASV.

31

proposals made by the great scholars, the simplest would be that the past tense refers to the portion of the epistle already completed.[12]

But why the repetition? I do not have a clue.

The assurances are addressed to different groups, but how many groups? "Little children" is applied to all John's readers throughout the epistle (2:1, 18, 28; 3:7, 18; 4:4; 5:21), and it is probably the same here. John relates to all of them as a teacher to his students or a spiritual father to his converts (cf. 1 Cor. 4:14–15).[13] But some were old and some were young. So John divides them into two groups. He calls some "fathers" and some "young men."

The two assurances addressed to "little children," including all the readers, are worded differently: "I write unto you, little children, because your sins are forgiven you[14] for his name's sake" (12); and: "I wrote unto you, little children, because you know the Father" (13c). *His name* refers to Christ Jesus and stands for who he is, all that he is (cf. 1:7; 2:1–2). Not for the sake of their own good works, but on account of his name they have been forgiven.

They are also assured that they know the Father—i. e., they have this intimate relationship with the Father. Compare the discussion of verses 4–6, where, however, the reference is most likely to the Son. In fact John is very plain that one can only enter into this relationship

---

[12] Robert Law points out that a writer may use either the present tense or the past with regard to a work in progress, depending on whether he is thinking of "his own immediate point of view" or "placing himself at his reader's point of view" when the letter is received. But why change from one to the other and why then repeat what he has just said? He thinks John may have been interrupted after writing the three present tenses; and then, when he returned to his work, resumed the thought by repeating what he had just written, but using a past tense instead of the present (*The Tests of Life*, 308f).

[13] Grk *teknion* is a diminutive of *teknon*, hence the plural *teknia* is "little children," in the New Testament "a term of kindly address by teachers to their disciples" (GT, 617). The second occurrence (13c), however, is from *paidia*, plural of *paidion*, which is a diminutive of *pais*.

[14] Or "have been forgiven you." The Greek is a perfect tense, which refers to something done in the past that continues to be effective in the present. It would seem to refer to the time of conversion as the point in the past where forgiveness first took place.

with the Father through the revelation he has made of himself in the Son (cf. 2:23; 5:20; 2 John 9).

The assurance to fathers, the older disciples, is exactly the same in each case: "you know him who is from the beginning" (13a, 14a). The reference is to Christ Jesus. What point would there be in identifying the Father as "him who is from the beginning"? No one denied it.

The address to young men is especially appropriate to them as being young and strong: "I write unto you, young men, because you have overcome the evil one," i. e. Satan, the devil (13b; cf. 3:7–12; 5:18–19); and then: "because you are strong, and the word of God remains in you, and you have overcome the evil one" (14b), indicating the source of the strength by which they overcame the evil one. The language could well apply to the time when they first overcame the world at their conversion (cf. 5:3–5). But perhaps it may also have reference to the controversy precipitated by the rise of the antichrists (2:18–27; 4:1–6).

So John has no doubt of the spiritual status of his readers. But even these of unquestioned spiritual standing could profit from a warning with regard to the seductive power of the world.

Warning Against Love of the World (15–17)

1. Connection of Thought. John's readers having the spiritual standing that they have, having been forgiven of their sins, having overcome the evil one, knowing God as they do, they are warned against love of the world. Such a warning would be pointless and useless if addressed to people whose existence derives from the world, whose teachers spoke the talk of the world, and who in fact could be identified with the world (4:5; cf. 3:1c); people who did not know the children of God because they did not know God (3:1c); who in fact hated the brethren (3:13). What would be the use warning them not to love the world, when in fact they were identified with the world? But John's readers had overcome the world through their faith in Jesus Christ (5:4–5). Like the apostles themselves (John 15:19; 17:14–16) John's readers had been separated from the world; though they were in the world, they were not of the world; their spiritual existence derived from God; they were of God, and knowing God, they would pay attention to those who spoke for God (4:6). It was such as they who could be warned not to be sucked in by the seductive power of the world; not to be enamored of the world, to be captivated by the siren sound which is the voice of the world.

33

2. Meaning of "the World." As we did when we sought to understand the metaphor of light and darkness, now again we must turn to the writings of John to understand what he means by "the world."

The Word had come into the world, but though "he was in the world, and the world was made through him," yet the world did not recognize him (John 1:10).

The world hated Jesus because he exposed its works as evil, but could not hate those who belonged to the world and posed no threat to its existence (John 7:7).

Jesus told unbelieving Jews: "You are from beneath; I am from above; you are of this world; I am not of this world" (John 8:23).

The cross was a judgment on the world, in which the ruler of the world, referring to Satan, would be cast out (John 12:31). By being lifted up on the cross Jesus would "draw all men" unto himself, thus building a new kingdom on the ruins of the old (John 12:32). Satan is also identified as the ruler of the world in John 14:30 & 16:11.

Jesus told the apostles they should not be surprised if the world hated them, for it had hated him. "If you were of the world, the world would love its own; but because you are not of the world, but I chose you out of the world, therefore the world hates you" (John 15:18–19).

The testimony of the Spirit would vindicate Christ Jesus and condemn the world (John 16:8–11; cf. 15:26–27).

The world would rejoice at the death of Jesus (John 16:20). But Jesus has overcome the world (John 16:33).

The revelation of the Father given to the apostles had separated them from the world, and the world hated them, because they were not of the world, even as he was not of the world (John 17:14–16).

Jesus' kingdom was "not of this world" (John 18:36).

Love of the world cannot coexist with love of the Father (1 John 2:15). The reason is, "all that is in the world ... is not of the Father, but is of the world" (v. 16). The world is temporal; it passes away (v. 17).

The world does not recognize children of God, just as it did not know God himself (1 John 3:1). The children of God must not be surprised if the world hates them (1 John 3:13).

False prophets are "of the world" and speak the language of the world, for which reason the world listens to them (1 John 4:5). "We," the witnesses of Christ (cf. 1:1–4), on the other hand, "are of God: he that knows God hears us; he who is not of God hears us not" (1 John 4:6).

By their faith the children of God have overcome the world (1 John 5:4–5).

"We know that we are of God, and the whole world lies in the evil one" (1 John 5:19); i. e., it is his domain, under his rule.

So "the world" refers to the old regime, under the rule of Satan. It is that regime which Jesus came to destroy, on the ruins of which he would build his kingdom. It is not the world as divinely created (John 1:10), as loved by God, which the Son was sent to save (John 3:16–17; 1 John 2:2; 4:9–14); but the world as in rebellion against its Creator, under the rule of the evil one (1 John 5:19), the world as the enemy of God's children (1 John 3:1c, 13).

Therefore, John warns those who have come to know God: "Love not the world, neither the things that are in the world."

3. Reasons (15b–17). John explains why his readers should heed his warning.

(1) The love of the world is incompatible with love of the Father (15b): "If any man love the world, the love of the Father is not in him." The two simply cannot coexist in the same person. This first explanation is then elaborated by means of a second:

(2) "For[15] all that is in the world ... is not of the Father, but is of the world" (16).[16]

John explains what he means by the things that are in the world. *The lust of the flesh* refers to desire that arises from human appetites. Neither of the terms John uses is in itself evil. The word *epithumia* (lust) can refer to legitimate desire (as in Luke 22:15 & Phil. 1:23); and the flesh is used of human nature without the evil often associated with it (John 1:14). Thus the desire for food, drink and sex are legitimate, in fact "all that satisfies the needs and wants of human beings taken as such" (Brown, 310). But legitimate desire can be perverted and cor-

---

[15] Grk *hoti*, because.

[16] The preposition *ek* means "out of." The things that are in the world do not have their source in the Father, but in the world.

rupted into something that serves the will of Satan rather than the will of God (as in Gen. 3:6 and Matt. 4:3), in which case it "is not of the Father, but is of the world."

The lust of the eyes is desire that arises from the sight. We see a thing and desire it. Eve "saw that the tree was good for food, and that it was a delight to the eyes" (Gen. 3:6). The devil showed Jesus "all the kingdoms of the world, and the glory of them" (Matt. 4:8). One's eye can cause him to stumble (Mark 9:47). Potiphar's wife "cast her eyes upon Joseph" and wanted him sexually (Gen. 39:7; cf. Job 31:1; Matt. 5:28). David "saw a woman bathing; and the woman was very beautiful to look upon" (2 Sam. 11:2), and the sight created desire for her. Peter's word portrait of false teachers included "having eyes full of adultery" (literally, an adulteress) (2 Pet. 2:14). But one can cast his eyes upon other things with the result of having desire stimulated. Thus Achan "saw" the wealth of Jericho, and then "coveted" and "took" (Josh. 7:21).

The first two elements deal with the sources from which desire arises. The third deals with pride of possession: *the pride of life*. Start with the Greek for life. It is not the word *zoe* (used in 1:1f), but the word *bios*, which also occurs in 3:17, where John speaks of one having "the *bion* (goods, possessions) of the world." It refers to the means of life, one's livelihood. It has the same sense in Mark 12:44 and Luke 21:4 where the widow cast into the treasury "all that she had, all her living"—i. e., all she had to live on; and in Luke 15:12 & 30, which speaks of the "living" divided among the two sons.

The Greek *alazoneia* only occurs elsewhere in the New Testament at James 4:16. Businessmen are challenged about all their great plans. Instead of speaking with understanding of their utter dependence upon the providential will of God, they act as if everything only depended upon themselves. James says: "you boast in your *alazoneiais*"—i. e., prideful, arrogant presumption. GT, 25 defines the combination of words in First John 2:16 as "display in one's style of living."

The related word *alazon* (in Rom. 1:30 & 2 Tim. 3:2) refers to a braggart. "The *alazon* is the one who 'makes more of himself' than the reality justifies. ... In First John 2:16 *alazoneia* denotes the attitude of the cosmic man who does not ask concerning the will of the Father but tries to make out that he himself may sovereignly decide concerning the shape of his life, whereas in actuality the decision lies with God, as is seen in the passing away of the world (v. 17). This is worked out with an example in James 4:16, where *alazoneiai* are expressions of the *alazoneia* which acts as if it could dispose of the future, whereas this is really under the control of the will of God (v. 15)" (Delling in TDNT, I, 226f).

Delling may have been unduly influenced by the use of this word in James 4:16. But he seems to be right about the unreality of the attitude toward this world's goods.[17] One can make more of these things than is justified. It is all a fake. It is like elevator shoes, hair pieces and the fronts of buildings on the set of a cheap western movie. The reality is other than appears to be the case. Such is John's assessment of worldly possessions. It is not what it appears to be.

(3) The third reason for heeding John's warning about love of the world is the impermanence of all things worldly: "And the world passes away, and the lust of it; but he that does the will of God abides for ever" (v. 17).

John had already written that "the darkness" was passing away, vanishing before the shining of the true light (v. 8). So also of the world system under the control of Satan and all things connected with it. Only the will and purpose of the Creator has permanence, and the survivors of the present world order will be only those who fulfill God's purpose for them.[18]

---

[17] Compare also the discussion in R. C. Trench, *Synonyms*, 98ff.

[18] "Permanent value attaches only to such things as correspond to God's plan for the world and for men. He that fulfils God's destiny for himself 'abideth for ever.' 'In the mind of God, values are facts, and indestructible facts. Whatever has value in God's sight is safe for evermore; time and change cannot touch it'" (Brooke in ICC).

━ FIRST JOHN 2:18–27 ━
Warning About Antichrist

The second passage about false prophets (4:1–6) would seem to establish a connection between the present warning and the previous warning about love of the world. The false prophets are said to be "of the world," for which reason they speak the language of the world "and the world hears them" (4:5). So we see why the warning against love of the world is followed by a warning against the false teachers.

John's second epistle also deals with this subject. John warns about deceivers who have gone out into the world; he warns against making common cause with such teachers who may come but who do not bring "the teaching of Christ" (2 John 7–11). As Acts 15 speaks of certain teachers who "came down from (Grk *apo*) Judea" (v. 1) and of "certain who went out from (Grk *ek*) us" (v. 24), and Galatians 2:12 of certain who "came from (also Grk *apo*) James," so John says, the teachers of which he warns "went out from us," literally *out of* us (Grk *ek*).[19]   But John's readers were to make no mistake about it. "They were not of (again Grk *ek*) us." The first *ek* seems to refer to a physical relationship and the second to a spiritual relationship. See further on this matter at verse 19.

As in 4:1–6, John speaks of three groups, "they," "us" and "you." The "us" refers to John and his colleagues, the original witnesses of Christ (1:1–4). The false teachers seem to have been associated with apostolic teachers, but had left their company, and John wanted his readers to understand that they did not belong to the apostolic fellowship. They did not abide in the teaching of Christ (2 John 9), nor did they "hear" the apostolic witnesses (1 John 4:6), and John was not about to place his endorsement upon them (cf. 2 John 7–11). He disowns them and their teaching, just as the Judaizers were disowned by the apostles and elders, and in fact the whole Jerusalem church (Acts 15:22–24). John reminds his readers of the truth they had been taught "from the beginning," which would enable them to recognize the deceivers as the liars they were, to deal with their teaching in the right way, and thus to remain true to the apostolic testimony about Christ Jesus.

---

[19] Compare also Acts 20:30, "and from among (Grk *ek*) your own selves shall men arise."

Rise of Antichrists the Certain Evidence of Coming Crisis (18–19)

John had supported his warning against love of the world by reference to its impermanence: "the world passes away, and its lusts" (17). Now he declares: "it is the last hour" (18a). The expression seems to be connected with the manifestation and the presence of Christ (in 28), and some scholars explain "the last hour" as having reference to the second coming of Christ and the end of history,[20] some (such as Raymond Brown) holding that John was in error. But those, like myself, who hold that the apostles spoke without error, will find this view unacceptable. It seems more likely that John may be referring to the passing of the Jewish age and the destruction of Jerusalem (cf. Matt. 24:3 in context). In fact we shall see below that the evidence by which John recognizes "that it is the last hour" has connections with Jesus' prophecy about the destruction of Jerusalem.

Proof that "it is the last hour" is found in the rise of "many antichrists" (18bc). The readers had heard "that antichrist comes." In fact Jesus himself had given advance warning to his apostles that "false Christs and false prophets" would arise in connection with the passing of the Jewish age (Matt. 24:5, 11, 24; Mark 13:21–23). Paul also had warned of "grievous wolves" who would enter in, "not sparing the flock" and of men who would arise from the church itself, "speaking perverse things, to draw away the disciples after them" (Acts 20:28–30).

The expectation of antichrist has now been realized, John writes, in the rise of "many antichrists" (cf. 4:1–3; 2 John 7). The singular "antichrist" does not refer to a single individual. According to John's interpretation, the singular must be understood as a collective, and to refer to anyone of this class, who rises up in opposition to Christ.[21]

John will soon identify the antichrists he has in mind more specifically (22–23; cf. 4:2–3 & 2 John 7). But here he simply appeals to the rise of "many antichrists" as evidence "that it is the last hour."

---

[20] Some drawing attention to passages (such as John 4:21, 5:25 & 16:2), in which an "hour" refers to an extended period.

[21] *Antichrist* means against Christ, and perhaps even in place of Christ, which would establish an even stronger connection with Jesus' prophecy which is cited above. The preposition *anti* has the meaning in place of or instead of.

John provides a description of their rise (in 19): "They went out from us," he writes, the *us* referring to himself and his colleagues, the apostolic witnesses (as in 4:6). The preposition *ek* is literally "out of," but the connection with the apostolic company was only physical (as in Acts 15:24), for John goes on to say: "but they were not of (*ek* again) us." The connection was only physical, whatever these teachers may have claimed; they did not derive from the apostles spiritually. As John will later say, "They are of (Grk *ek*) the world." John wants his readers to understand that these teachers were not sent out with the endorsement of the apostles.

Had they been "of us," John continues, "they would have continued with us" (19b). But they did not remain in the fellowship of the apostles, as John will urge his readers to do (24), and their exodus from the company of true teachers is a certain manifestation "that they all are not of (Grk *ek*) us." Without a single exception! Not one of them derives from the apostolic company.

Assurance: Proof Against the Antichrists (20–21)

"And you," writes John, with emphasis in the Greek: *you* in contrast to the antichrists, "have an anointing from the Holy One." Jesus was anointed with the Holy Spirit and with power (Acts 10:38 with Isaiah 11:2; 42:1; Matt. 3:16; 12:15–28). The Spirit was upon Jesus because he had been anointed to preach (Luke 4:18, quoting Isaiah 61:1f). Paul and his associates had been anointed by God, and this anointing is connected with the seal and earnest of the Spirit (2 Cor. 1:21).

The consequence of the anointing, John assures his readers, is knowledge of the truth: "and you know all things"—everything you need to know. "Some very ancient authorities read *and you all know*" (ASV margin), i. e., you all have knowledge. The latter may be the original reading, since it seems more likely that a scribe may have felt the need to supply an object to the verb *know*, than that the reading with the object *all things* should be changed to the other reading without the object, which is a more difficult reading. So I am inclined to the view that John is assuring his readers that in consequence of the anointing they all have knowledge. The object will then be clarified by the next verse (21).

The consequence of the anointing, therefore, links it to promises which had been specially addressed to the apostles. Consider two of the promises: "These things have I spoken to you, while abiding with you. But the Comforter (or Helper), the Holy Spirit, whom the Father will send in my name, he shall teach you all things, and bring to your remembrance all that I said to you" (John 14:25–26). Clearly this promise is specially addressed to the apostles as men who had experienced the personal presence and teaching of Jesus. Peter would later anticipate the need of doing something to make it possible for Christians who were not eyewitnesses to remember the truth (2 Pet. 1:12–15). What he does is put the truth into writing (2 Pet. 3:1).

Then Jesus promised the apostolic witnesses, who had been with him from the beginning (John 15:26–27), that the Holy Spirit would guide them "into all the truth" (John 16:12–15).

The possession of the "anointing" by John's readers must be explained from everything that is known about the manifestation of the Spirit. As we have seen, Jesus made special promises to the apostles about the coming of the Spirit upon them to equip them for their task (John 14:25–26 in contrast with 2 Pet. 1:12–15 & 3:1; John 15:26–26; 16:12–15). When we turn to the book of Acts we find the Holy Spirit coming upon the apostles (chs. 1–2) and then being communicated to others by the apostles through the laying on of their hands (Acts 8:14–19; 19:1–6).

The persons addressed in First John had been taught by the anointing (1 John 2:20–21; cf. v. 27). But how? Evidence on this point is provided later. Consider the way 3:24b is immediately followed by 4:1. John first assures his readers: "And hereby we know that he abides in us, by the Spirit which he gave us" (3:24b). But that assurance is immediately followed by a caution: "Beloved, believe not every spirit, but prove the spirits, whether they are of God, because many false prophets are gone out into the world" (4:1). We expect the explanation to be: "because many false spirits are gone out into the world." But John writes "many false prophets" instead. The caution in 4:1 explains the way in which the Spirit had been given (3:24b). It was not that the anointing of the Spirit made each Christian a prophet, each hearing voices from God, but John's readers had the Spirit through the presence of prophets among them.

Then notice further that the teaching derived from this anointing with the Spirit is not new truth, but that which had been heard from the beginning (2:24 with 2:27).

John continues: "I have not written to you because you do not know the truth, but because you know it, and because no lie is of the truth" (21). His readers were already equipped with knowledge of the truth. John is simply putting into writing what they already knew. He had no fear his readers would not be able to recognize the antichrists when they appeared. They just needed to draw upon the truth which they already knew and to realize that "no lie is of the truth." It is not some new aspect or interpretation of the truth. It is a lie, pure and simple.

Recognizing the Antichrist by Making Use of the Truth Already Known (22–23)

John raises the question: "Who is the liar but he that denies that Jesus is the Christ?" (22a). He continues by asserting that the one who denies that Jesus is the Christ (22a) is not only "the liar" par excellence, but also "the antichrist" who denies both the Father and the Son (22b).

Now if these teachers would be inclined to claim that they only denied the Son and not the Father, John replies that one cannot have the Father without the Son: "Whosoever denies the Son, the same does not have the Father; he that confesses the Son has the Father also" (23). Again we have a verse that is explained by a later passage. The epistle closes with the assertion that we know the true God and Father through the revelation he has made of himself in his Son (5:20). The prologue to the Gospel of John speaks of "the Word" that reveals God; he "became flesh" (John 1:14) and through him the invisible God has been made known (v. 18). Throughout the Gospel of John we find Jesus claiming that he speaks the words of the Father and does the works of the Father, thus revealing the Father (John 5:19–20, 36; 7:16–17; 8:28; 10:25, 32; 12:48–50). Finally, the night before the crucifixion he claims: "I am the way, and the truth, and the life: no one comes to the Father, but by me" (14:6). He expresses impatience with Philip because even after so long he did not recognize that the Father was made known in the Son. "He that has seen me has seen the Father" (14:7–9). It is not that the two were one personality (for see 1:1 and many other places throughout John), but that the Father has been revealed through the Son. For that reason, one cannot have the Father without the Son.

Counsel to the Readers with Regard to the Deceivers (24–27)

The readers' security against apostasy lies in keeping the thing they had heard from the beginning (24): "As for you,[22] let that remain in you which you heard from the beginning. If that which you heard from the beginning remains in you, you also shall remain in the Son, and in the Father."

The anointing, then, is not a matter of an inward voice continually speaking new truth. New revelation was not needed, but simply to let the old truth, which is tantamount to the truth taught in the Gospel of John, remain within and guide them.

John continues: "And this is the promise which he promised us, the life eternal" (25). The scholarly commentators debate whether *this* points backward to what John has just said (24) or forward to *the life eternal*. The statement seems abrupt if it has no reference to what has preceded, and perhaps we should be guided by later references which explain that eternal life is "in the Son" and the one who "has the Son has the life" (5:11–12; cf. 13, 20). The word *promise* only occurs here in John's writings. But the Gospel is filled with references to the promise of eternal life without using the word, and with the idea that to have the Son is to have eternal life (John 1:4; 3:14–16; 3:36; 5:21–26; 6:40, 47–51, 53–58, 63, 68; 8:51; 11:25–26; 15:4). Consider especially the explanation in Jesus' prayer: "And this is life eternal, that they should know you the only true God, and him whom you did send, Jesus Christ" (17:3).

So it would seem that *this* looks both ways, and verse 25 can be summarized thus: "And this—i. e., the relationship with deity set forth in verse 24—is the promise which he promised us, and this relationship amounts to the life eternal." That, in fact, is what is at stake in the present controversy.

John then summarizes his subject: "These things have I written to you concerning them that would lead you astray (or deceive you)" (26).[23] They have departed from the apostolic fellowship (19) and they are out to recruit others. With so much at stake, John has explained the issues so that his readers will be motivated to remain with the original apostolic teaching.

---

[22] Again the *you* is emphatic in Greek.

[23] See footnote on 1:8 for the Greek *planao*.

The development of the thought closes with another reference to the security they can have through the anointing received from Christ Jesus: "And as for you,[24] the anointing which you received of him remains in you, and you need not that any one teach you; but as his anointing teaches you concerning all things, and is true, and is no lie, and even as it taught you, you abide in him" (27).

Observe several points:

(1) The anointing remains as that which they heard from the beginning remains (24).

(2) This teaching is sufficient. They had no need of a teacher, not even the apostle himself, since they already knew the truth (21), and certainly not a teacher who had broken fellowship with the apostles (19). John is not teaching them something that they did not know, but merely putting into writing what they had already heard by word of mouth (cf. 1:3–4).

(3) The present teaching of the anointing ("teaches you") is merely what was taught ("even as it taught you") from the beginning (cf. 24).

(4) Again, they have no need of continual new teaching, but only continual listening to the old teaching—the thing they had heard from the beginning.

So it is today. The apostles were guided into all the truth and they have put that truth into writing. We have no need of new teachers, but need only to stay with the apostolic testimony, to let it remain in us and guide us.

---

[24] Again emphatic.

FIRST JOHN 2:28–3:12
Righteousness as a Distinguishing Mark of the Children of God

Determining the "break points" in this epistle is notoriously difficult. The ASV prints 2:28–29 as a continuation of the previous passage, indicates a distinct break between 2:28–29 and 3:1 and a new beginning at 3:1. The Greek Testament from the United Bible Societies, on the other hand, indicates a new beginning at 2:28 and a close connection between 2:28–29 and 3:1–10.

The matter can be pretty subjective. But I incline to the view that the new address "little children" (2:28) marks a transition to a new development. In fact, 2:28–29 seems transitional, being linked by some of its language to the preceding passage, but at the same time introducing a new thought which will be developed at some length. That is John's way. The conclusion of one passage will often introduce a new thought, which is to be developed in the next passage, but then he will come back and relate the new thought to what has already been presented. So it is here.

As was the case with the previous passage (2:26), this one also arises out of the author's concern about deceivers (3:7). He does not want his "little children" to be led astray by a liar (cf. 2:4, 22).

Transitional Passage Introducing the New Thought of Doing Righteousness as an Identifying Mark of Children of God (2:28–29)

The new address to John's "little children" begins with an exhortation to remain in God (or Christ)[25] in view of his future manifestation (2:28). The exhortation: "remain in him" links the new beginning to the previous passage. John has already explained how one remains in

---

[25] One of the repeated difficulties in First John is determining whether "he" and "him" refers to God the Father or to Christ the Son. But this difficulty will not seem as consequential when we keep in mind that John continually thinks of God as manifested in Christ (cf. esp. 5:20). So one concept is never very far from the other.

45

Christ (cf. 2:27 with 24). His readers will abide in both the Son and the Father if they allow the teaching which they heard from the beginning to remain in them.[26]

A purpose clause (28b) is attached to the exhortation: *that, if he shall be manifested, we may have boldness, and not be ashamed before him at his coming* (or *presence*). The "if" in "if he shall be manifested" is conditional only as to time. His manifestation is not in doubt, but only its time.

The positive aspect of the purpose is "that we may have boldness." The Greek *parrhesia* refers to freedom of speech (cf. 3:21 & 5:14) and then confidence in general (GT, 491; AG, 630). Here the definition is sharpened by the addition of a negative aspect: "and not be ashamed from him at his presence." The preposition *apo* is actually *from* rather than *before*. That is why GT, 17 (on *aischuno*) explains the clause: "that we may not in shame shrink from him." The idea of being put to shame or experiencing disgrace is also found in the Old Testament with reference to Jehovah's appearance in judgment (Is. 1:29; Jer. 12:13).

The Greek *parousia* is more literally *presence*, as is clear at First Cor. 16:17, Philippians 2:12 and Second Cor. 10:10. "The use of *parousia* as a technical term has developed in two directions. On the one hand the word served as a cult expression for the coming of a hidden divinity, who makes his presence felt by a revelation of his power, or whose presence is celebrated in the cult. ... On the other hand, *parousia* became the official term for a visit of a person of high rank; especially of kings and emperors visiting a province" (AG, 630, which see for references).

The assurance possessed by John's "little children" (29) is brought in pretty abruptly, and the connection is difficult to make out. But 3:6 indicates a link between doing righteousness and abiding in Christ. That would seem to explain the connection between 2:28 and 2:29. The exhortation to abide in him (28) leads on to an assurance with regard to those who practice righteousness: *If you know that he is righteous, you know* (or *know you,* taking the verb imperatively as it could be) *that every one also that does righteousness is begotten of him* (29).

---

[26] The exhortation: "remain in him," which stands at the beginning of the next major passage, is a condition proving from the outset that nothing in the succeeding passage can teach unconditional security.

First the conditional element: "If you know that he is righteous." Do you know that God as manifested in Christ is righteous? Yes. Every Christian knows that. Very well. Then if you think about it for just a moment you will realize that you also possess some additional knowledge which follows from that fact, namely, "that every one who does righteousness is begotten of him." The one who does righteousness manifests a kinship with God. He shows that he has been begotten of God and is therefore a child of God.

Notice what John says and does not say. He does not say: "Every one that is begotten of God does righteousness," although that would be true as well. What he does say is: "Everyone who does righteousness is begotten of him." The point is that one who does righteousness gives evidence of being a child of God.

That is the new point that is introduced at the end of Chapter 2: *Doing Righteousness as an Identifying Characteristic of the Children of God*, which will be elaborated in Chapter 3. Again John will be drawing lines between the children of God and the children of the devil.

Children of God, Present Position and Future Hope (3:1–2)

The idea of being begotten of God (2:29) leads to this reflection upon the marvel of divine love that has made us children of God.

1. The Marvelous Love That Makes Us Children of God (1a).

The sentence begins with an exclamation: "Behold!" or "Look!" the word calling attention to something extraordinary, something marvelous to see. That marvel is the sort of love the Father has bestowed on us. The Greek *potapos* means "of what sort or quality" (GT, 533) or "of what sort or kind" (AG, 694). As in the disciples' marveling over the magnificence of the temple, its stones and structure (Mark 13:1), so here, context calls for the meaning "how great, how wonderful" or "how glorious" (AG, 695).

"Look! What magnificent love the Father has bestowed on us, that we should be called children of God!" But the connecting word is not *hoti*, but *hina*: "that," but indicating aim or purpose, "in order that." So the point is the greatness of the love that made it possible for us to be called children of God. John will twice return to this point: "Hereby know we love, because he laid down his life for us" (3:16). "Herein was the love of God manifested in us, that (Grk *hoti*) God has sent his only begotten Son into the world that we might live through him. Herein is love, not that we loved God, but that he loved us, and sent his Son as the propitiation for our sins" (4:9–10).

We are "called" children of God. God has owned us as his children, which makes us his legitimate children. "And," John adds, "we are." Calling us "children of God" is no empty pretense, no "legal fiction." What we are called we actually "are."

2. Explanation of Non-recognition by the World (1b).

Our identity and relation to God is precisely the reason the unregenerated world does not recognize us, a point to which John will return at verse 13. The world does not know us, and even manifests hostility toward us. But it is not surprising. The world did not know God, and it is precisely for that reason that it does not know his children. In fact, it would be a bad sign were the world to heap its accolades upon us.

3. Hope for the Future (2).

"Now we are children of God, and it is not yet made manifest what we shall be" (2a). It is not that we shall become something other than children of God, but that we will ultimately share the glory of Christ (Rom. 8:16–17; Phil. 3:21). But that glory which shall eventually be manifested toward us has not yet been revealed (Rom. 8:18–19). So our identity is for the time being, as it were, shrouded with a veil.

We do, however, have limited knowledge with regard to the future state: "We know that, if he[27] shall be manifested, we shall be like him; because (Grk *hoti*) we shall see him even as he is" (2b). The explanation is ambiguous. Does it mean that likeness to him is a condition of seeing him? (cf. Matt. 5:8). Or is it that the sight of him will have a transforming effect on us? (cf. 2 Cor. 3:18).

I am not sure. But it may help to compare the prologue to the Gospel (John 1:1–18). God is unseen, but manifested in his Son, who became like us (vv. 14, 18). That manifestation has made it possible

---

[27] The Greek could as well be rendered "it (i. e., what we shall be) shall be manifested." But John has just spoken of the manifestation of Christ (2:28).

for us to become what we now are, children of God. Perhaps John is now saying that in order to see him we must become as he is.[28]

Bearing of This Hope on Present Practice (3:3–6)

John adds a statement with regard to the present practice of those who hold the hope he has just mentioned in verse 2: "And every one that has this hope set on him purifies himself, even as he is pure" (3). No one who entertains the hope John described in 2b can be morally indifferent. For what is that hope, but the hope of being like Christ? Do you have the hope of being "like him"? Is that what you want? Then you will live in a way that is compatible with that hope. Every single person that has this hope "purifies himself, even as he is pure." No other way of life is compatible with this hope.

The Greek for "purifies" is *hagnizo*; and for "pure," *hagnos*. The latter occurs in First Tim. 5:22 where the admonition not to "be partaker of other men's sins" is followed by another: "keep yourself pure." So to be pure is to be free from sin, and to purify oneself is to rid oneself of sin. The context that follows in First John (3:4–6) proves that the same implication applies here.

A person who has the hope of being like Christ in future endeavors to be like Christ in the present. He purifies himself, or makes himself pure. But if a child of God is continually endeavoring to purify himself, if indeed that is necessary, then he is not perfectly pure and free from sin in the present. That implication is consistent with what John has written in 1:8–2:2, and also has important bearing on the way the following verses must be interpreted.

Every one! All! Every one that has this hope purifies himself or makes himself pure. There are no exceptions. But what if a person does not live this way? What if, instead of battling against sin, he gives in to it and gives his life over to the practice of sin? John has several points to make in support of what he has said about the way of life of every person who has the hope of ultimately being like Christ.

---

[28] "What men saw of Jesus of Nazareth, when He manifested His glory under the limitations of human life, raised them to the position of children of God, in the case of all who received Him (John 1:13). How much greater transforming power shall there be in the vision of Him as He is, no longer veiled by the conditions of earthly life!" (Brooke).

1. The first point concerns the serious nature of his actions: "Every one that does sin does also lawlessness; and sin is lawlessness." That is what sin is. It is lawlessness. Every one that gives his life to sin is a lawless person. He ignores and disregards the law of God. Is this a person who entertains the hope of being like Christ?

2. Furthermore, his life contradicts both the mission and the character of Christ: "And you know that he was manifested to take away sins; and in him is no sin" (5). Can a person whose life is given to sin rather than to purification from sin, then, possibly be one of those whose hope is to be like Christ?

3. The last point (6) follows from what was said in verse 5: "Whosoever remains in him does not sin" (6a). The idea of remaining in Christ marks a return to the thought with which this section began. John had called upon his little children to remain in Christ in order that they may have boldness and not shrink from him in shame at his presence (2:28). Here he adds that a life of sin is inconsistent with a life lived in union with Christ.

The reverse side of this assertion with regard to the one who sins follows in 6b. The person given to sin is not abiding in Christ: "Whosoever sins has not seen him, neither has known him." John is not saying that a person cannot apostatize; that a person cannot abandon Christ and go back to the life of sin. He is not saying that the person who sins has never known him. It is important to notice the use of the perfect tense in both verbs. The perfect tense refers to something done in the past that continues to have its effect in the present. The person who lives a life of sin has not known Christ, so that this knowledge continues to have its effect in the present. Any knowledge he has had of Christ no longer has its effect, so that he continues to know him in the present. If he has previously known him, then a life of sin represents a renunciation of all that he had experienced.

Verse 6 cannot be understood to mean that a Christian has no sin (cf. 1:8). That would be inconsistent with the way this development of thought began in verse 3, where John says the person who has the hope defined in verse 2 purifies himself. He is not perfectly pure as yet, but he strives to make himself pure and free from sin.

That being so, then verse 6 cannot mean he has no sin from which he needs to be purified. Nor would such a view be consistent with what John wrote in 1:8–2:2.

The meaning of the whole section (3–6) will be understood if we recall how John defined his purpose in 2:1a. "These things write I unto you that you may not sin." The immediate context relates to what he had just said about being cleansed from sin by the blood of Christ (1:5–10). Nothing in what John had just said should cause one to take sin lightly. His purpose was not to encourage them to take a casual view of sin. His purpose was to encourage them not to sin.

Although the context is different here, John's purpose is the same. He writes what he does, not to assure his readers that they had no sin (contrary to what he had written in 1:8), but to give reasons for them to avoid sin. To take sin lightly, to give oneself over to the practice of sin, would be inconsistent with their entire position in Christ. It would be a contradiction of the hope they entertained (3). It would be to give themselves to lawlessness (4). It would go against the mission of Christ and the character of Christ (5). It would be a complete contradiction of their position in Christ (6). John is not assuring his readers that they have no sin. He is giving reasons not to sin.

But they were threatened by morally indifferent teachers who would deceive them on this point, who evidently took the position that one need not worry about sin. One could be righteous without leading a righteous life. That is the point to which John now turns.

Warning Against Deception on This Subject (3:7–12)

John warns his little children: "Let no man deceive you (or lead you astray)" (7a). The explanations that follow make the matter plain. John is warning about morally indifferent teachers who claim to be above morality. They were teaching that one could be righteous without practicing what is right. But John will not permit his little children to be deceived. He makes the matter so plain that no one need be deceived: "He that does righteousness is righteous, even as he is righteous" (7b). On the other hand, the one who practices sin is not righteous, but derives his spiritual existence from[29] the devil (8a). The

---

[29] Greek *ek*, out of.

proof (Grk *hoti*) is that "the devil sins from the beginning" (8b). He has always sinned, at least from the beginning of history (cf. Gen. 3). So one who lives a life of sin is no child of God, but shows himself to be akin to the devil. The purpose and aim of the manifestation of the Son of God was to "destroy the works of the devil" (8c). Plainly, one who gives himself to sin goes against the mission of the Son of God, and certainly is not righteous.

Verse 7b is John's second assertion about "one who does righteousness." The development of thought in this section had started with an inference drawn from the knowledge that God is righteous: "you know that every one also that does righteousness is begotten of him" (2:29). Now he takes the thought a step further: "Everyone who is begotten of God does not do sin" (9a, attempt at literal translation). The assertion rules out any exceptions. The reason (Grk *hoti*) one who is begotten of God does not sin is that God's seed remains in him (9a), having been planted in him through the preaching of the gospel (Jas. 1:18; 1 Pet. 1:22–25) and imparts the divine nature to him.

But John adds another assertion: "and he cannot sin, because he is begotten of God" (9b). The statement is not an absolute, but a conditional impossibility, as in other passages in the Gospel of John where the same language is used. For example: "How can you believe, who receive glory one of another, and the glory from the only God you do not seek?" (John 5:44). Jesus did not mean belief was absolutely impossible, but it was impossible under the circumstances.

Another example: "You cannot hear my word" (John 8:43b). Not that it was absolutely impossible, but that it was impossible while their will was to do the desires of their father the devil (v. 44).

Again: "For this cause they could not believe" (John 12:39). Again the impossibility was only conditional and not absolute, and in fact "even of the rulers many believed on him" (v. 42).

The "cannot" in First John 3:9b is only a conditional and not an absolute impossibility. John means that the one begotten of God cannot sin without going against all that he is and forfeiting his standing as a child of God. John certainly would not have warned his little children against being deceived by someone who held that one need not do righteousness in order to be righteous (v. 7) if after all it was impossible for them to do otherwise. Again he is providing reasons for them to purify themselves (3:3) and to avoid sin (2:1a); not teaching them not to worry about sin.

So again we see that John is not contradicting what he had already said (1:8–10), but is executing the intention he set forth in 2:1a. He is not claiming that children of God "have no sin," but writing what he does about the conflict between being begotten of God and living in sin, so that children of God may be strongly encouraged to avoid sin.

Verses 10–12, like 2:28–29, serve a dual function. On the one hand, they summarize what has been said in verses 7–9, the line that is clearly drawn between children of God and children of the devil, refuting those who claim that one may be righteous without living a life of righteousness. On the other, by specifying a particular, and in fact, the outstanding manifestation of righteousness, love of one's brother, they introduce the next development of thought (discussed in 3:13–24).

The scholarly commentaries debate to no great consequence whether *in this*, which stands at the beginning of verse 10, is referring to what has just been said (7–9) or to what is about to be said (10b). I say *to no great consequence* because the point is going to be the same either way. Both before and after 10a John is showing where the line is drawn between children of God and children of the devil. The test that he applies here makes both *manifest*. So no one need be confused. No one need be deceived. Since John is refuting those who hold that one may be righteous without doing righteousness, or be a child of God while living a life of sin, the test is summarized negatively in 10b. He had started out the subsection by saying against his opponents: *he that does righteousness is righteous* (7b). He now closes out the discussion by asserting the negative corollary: *everyone who does not practice righteousness is not of God* (10b). Furthermore, John had said: *he that practices sin is of the devil* (8a), and now implies: *everyone who does not practice righteousness is a child of the devil*. So the lines are so clearly drawn that no one need make any mistake or be deceived by one who claims otherwise.

When John adds: *neither he that does not love his brother* (10b), he specifies the outstanding manifestation of righteous living and thus introduces the new point which will be elaborated in what follows through verse 24. Thus verse 10 serves the same function as 2:28–29 in the structure of the epistle. John's method is to discuss

53

one topic, at the end of the discussion introducing a new point to be developed in the next section, eventually showing how all the points are intertwined.

Having introduced the new specific aspect of doing righteousness, love of one's brother (10b), John attaches an explanation: *For[30] this is the message which you heard from the beginning, that we should love one another; ...* (11). Again we see that the message *heard from the beginning* is that message which is preserved in the Gospel of John (cf. 13:34–35; 15:12–14, 17). The message (Grk *aggelia*, here and 1:5) had not only been declared (Grk *apaggello*) by word of mouth (1:3) but also put into writing (1:4). Thus the epistle seems to build upon the earlier writing of the same author.

A negative example is attached (in 12), perhaps the outstanding illustration of behavior that contradicts the duty to love one's brother: *not as Cain was of the evil one, and murdered[31] his brother.* John begins with a negative example illustrating the world's hatred (13). Soon he will add the outstanding positive example by which his readers may know what love is (16).

"For what reason,"[32] John asks, "did he murder him?" (12b). The answer lies in the great difference between the works of the children of God and the children of the devil, which John has already expounded: "Because his works were evil, but (Grk *de*) his brother's righteous" (12c). Genesis 4:1–8 tells the story, and indicates the great anger Cain felt because Jehovah had respect for Abel and his sacrifice, but had no respect for Cain and his offering. For that reason Cain was full of wrath, hated his brother and murdered him.

It seems clear that a climax is reached in the question of the reason Cain murdered Abel and its answer. The main point, therefore, is not that Cain murdered Abel, but the reason he did so. Cain is brought in

---

[30] Grk *hoti* = because.

[31] Grk *sphazo*: "to slaughter," butcher or murder (AG, 796; so also GT, 609). Both lexicons explain the present usage of putting to death or killing a person by violence. The verb is used for the slaughter of a lamb (Rev. 5:6, 9, 12; 13:8) and the violent killing of persons (Rev. 6:4, 9; 18:24). It is used in Rev. 13:3 of "a head that seemed to be mortally wounded" (AG). Only elsewhere here.

[32] Grk *charin* (AG, 877; GT, 665).

logically as a negative example because he stands as such a perfect type and model of the world and its antagonism toward the children of God. The children of God are comparable to Abel, with his righteous works. Cain was the first great example of the evil works and the hatred that characterizes the world in its opposition to the children of God (cf. John 3:19–21), and that brings John to his next subsection, which begins with a reference to the world's hatred of the children of God and then the great significance of love of the brothers, which marks the children of God.

The Application of the Subsection 2:28–3:12

This passage is certainly not intended to tell Christians that they need not be concerned about sin, or that they have no sin, since in fact it is impossible for them to sin. Rather to the contrary, John has written as he has in this section because it is possible for Christians to fall into sin (cf. 1:8–2:1). The passage is intended to encourage them to purify themselves, to warn them against sin and to give them the strongest possible reasons for avoiding sin.

Before everything else, the passage is a challenge to take righteous living seriously. It aims to make us realize that one cannot be a child of God and be careless about sin; for sin goes against everything that we are as children of God

FIRST JOHN 3:13–24
Love of the Brothers as Evidence of Life

In the previous section (2:28–3:12) John has discussed righteous living as a distinguishing mark by which the children of God may be recognized. This characteristic marks them as akin to God. On the other hand, when this characteristic is missing in a person's life he is not a child of God but a child of the devil, who is characterized by sin just as God is characterized by righteousness. So here is where the line is clearly drawn between children of God and children of the devil.

The development of thought has concluded with a special, in fact perhaps the principal manifestation of righteous living, namely love of the brothers (10–12). Now John is ready to develop that particular manifestation of righteous living and to point to love of the brothers as an unmistakable evidence of the right relationship with God (13–24). This type of development is characteristic of the structure of First John. The discussion of one point will conclude with the introduction of another, perhaps a special angle on the preceding point. This phenomena is also found at the end of the present passage (24b with 4:1–6). But John keeps coming back to previous points, and to indicate how all his points are actually one interrelated and connected whole. So the discussion gets broader and broader, but always keeping the previous elements and indicating the way all the points are connected. Some have spoken of this structure as a spiral.

The leading thought of the present passage is not new. John made substantially the same point about the significance of love of the brothers in 2:7–11. But the present passage is not just a repetition of the previous one. It has new elements. After pointing to love of the brothers as the evidence of life (13–15) John defines love in terms of the way it shows itself (16–17), argues that genuine love, being as it is a proof of one's relationship with God (and of the truth), quiets a troubled conscience (18–20), indicates the blessed fruit of an uncondemning conscience (21–22), explains the commandments, the keeping of which gives evidence of the relationship with God (23–24a) and, finally, indicates how we know that, namely, from the testimony of the Holy Spirit (24b).

Love of the Brothers the Ground of Knowledge of the Possession of Life (13–15)

The section begins by pointing out that the brothers should not be surprised if the world hates them (13). It has always been that way, going back to Cain, the archetypal worldling, who hated his brother (11–12). It is no great marvel, if Cain's spiritual descendants, also hate the children of God. The reason Cain hated and therefore killed his brother was emphatic and climactic in the previous passage. It was "because his works were evil, and his brother's righteous" (12b). And it is no different today. In fact, John has just pointed out that this is the way to tell the difference between children of God and children of the devil. One does righteousness and the other does evil. It certainly should not shock us, then, when, like Cain, the world hates us for the same reason as Cain killed Abel—i. e., because their works are evil and the works of the children of God are righteous.

The knowledge we have with regard to our spiritual position should take away the shock at the world's hatred. The very characteristic that distinguishes the children of God from the world and shows that they no longer belong to the world is love of the brothers: "We[33] know that we have passed out of death into life, because we love the brothers" (14a). The Greek verb *metabaino* means "to pass over from one place to another, to remove, depart" (GT, 404b) and here is used figuratively of moving from one realm to another. AG, 510b cites an extrabiblical usage of this verb with reference to a deceased person. A deceased person has moved from the realm of life to the realm of death. The same verb is used in John 5:24. The believer, said Jesus, "has eternal life, and comes not into judgment, but has passed out of death into life." In that verse the passing from death into life elaborates "eternal life."

Love of the brothers is not the condition upon which one moves from death to life, but the evidence of it. On the other hand, one who does not love, like Cain, "remains in death" (14b). Can anyone doubt it? Certainly not, when we understand the great guilt of hating one's brother. "Everyone that hates his brother is a murderer" (15a). The assertion is consistent with Jesus' teaching that the one who is angry

---

[33] Emphatic. The pronoun is expressed rather than being indicated only by the verb ending.

with his brother or treats him with contempt is liable to the punishment that is reserved for murderers (Matt. 5:21–22). One who hates his brother wishes that he might be rid of his brother. He might be restrained from the external act for various reasons, but he is a murderer at heart.

John adds that children of God know one thing about murderers: "You know that no murderer has eternal life remaining in him" (15b). Whatever may once have been true, eternal life does not remain in a murderer. From the patriarchal era the fate deserved by a murderer has been made manifest (Gen. 9:5–6). "You know" about murderers, says John.

Love Defined by the Manifestation of God in Christ (16–17)

Love is objectively and specifically defined. Love needs definition. John's "love" has nothing to do with the indefinite "love" manifested in the world. "In this we know love,"[34] writes John, "because he (literally that one)[35] laid down his life for us" (16a). This is how we know what love is. We know what hate, the opposite of love, is from the example of Cain (12). We know what love is from what happened at the cross. For the language "laid down" compare John 10:17–18,[36] where the voluntary act of laying down one's life is opposed to having one's life taken away. The Greek *tithemi* means to put down or to lay down. It is used at John 13:4 for the laying aside of one's garments. One has his life in hand, but lays it down or lays it aside.

An obligation follows, the obligation to manifest that same love toward the brothers: "and we ought to lay down our lives for the brothers" (16b). We do not know the circumstances John might have had in mind, but whatever occasion presents itself, in which we might save the life of our brothers by giving up our own, would be included. The obligation for disciples follows from the example of the Teacher: "He that says he remains in him ought himself also to walk even as he walked" (2:6). Jesus taught his disciples to love each other even as he loved them (John 13:34; 15:12–13).

That is the obligation following from the example and the teaching of Jesus. Now we may think we love our brothers in such heroic mea-

---

[34] Literally, *the love*. Whatever may parade under the name "love" in the world, John has in mind the genuine article that was manifested at the cross.

[35] Grk *ekeinos*.

[36] The Greek *tithemi* also occurs at John 10:11, 15; 13:37–38; 15:13.

sure. But the fact is, an occasion for laying down one's life for his brothers is extremely rare. The real test comes much more frequently in terms of the opportunity to give, not our lives, but our livelihoods. How does our love stand such a smaller test, but one more likely to occur? So John makes his application by raising a question in verse 17: "But whoever has worldly possessions, and beholds his brother having need, and locks up his compassion from him, how does the love of God remain in him?"

The situation has three characteristics:

1. A person has (Grk *echo*) something: "Whoever has the world's goods"—literally, *the life of the world*. The Greek for life is *bios*, as in 2:17, referring to the means of life, livelihood, as in Mark 12:44 & Luke 21:4; also Luke 15:12, 30. He has worldly possessions.

2. "He beholds his brother having (Grk *echo*) need" (literal translation). He observes that his brother has something too. He himself has worldly possessions. His brother has a need.

3. What does he do about the situation? "He locks up[37] his *splagchna* from him." The Greek *splagchna* is the plural of *splagchnon*, which is used literally in Acts 1:18 with reference to "inward parts, entrails"—in other words, one's "innards"; figuratively here "of the seat of the emotions, in our usage *heart*" (AG, 762). The KJV's "bowels" is a literal translation. GT, 584 defines the word as "bowels, intestines," including "the heart, lungs, liver, etc. ... In the Greek poets from Aeschyl. down the bowels were regarded as the seat of the more violent passions, such as anger and love; but by the Hebrews as the seat of the tenderer affections, esp. kindness, benevolence, compassion." But in English we use the word *heart* for the seat and center of the tender affections. We do not say: "I love you with all my guts," but: "I love you with all my heart."

Now here is the situation. A person has material goods. He sees a brother who does not have the world's goods, but has a need instead. But instead of letting compassion flow from his heart toward that brother, so as to help him with that need, he locks up his heart, so that compassion "is like a thing inaccessible to one" (GT on *kleio*, 348a).

Now here is what John wants to know: "How does the love of God remain in him?" It is plain to see that the love of God which was manifested at the cross (16a) is not in that person. We are called upon

---

[37] Greek *kleio*. The Greek for "key" is *kleis*.

to reproduce the love of God in ourselves, to love as we were loved, which is to say that "we ought to lay down our lives for the brothers." But if we lock up our hearts so that compassion cannot flow out to a brother in need by sharing our goods with him, then no way on earth can we possibly claim that the love of that one who laid down his life for us is in us. That is John's point.

Love as Providing Relief for a Troubled Conscience (18–20)

John has already taught us that love of the brothers, that genuine love that shows itself in self-sacrifice for our brothers, is evidence "that we have passed out of death into life," and are therefore in possession of eternal life (13–17; cf. John 5:24). He continues now along the same lines, reinforcing the same truth, but also indicating how this certainty with regard to life and the relationship with God has the consequence of providing peace for a troubled conscience. What a wonderful blessing comes from practicing love toward our brothers!

The thought begins with an exhortation, growing out of the previous subsection, to practice genuine love toward our brothers (18). The exhortation is addressed to John's spiritual children. "Let us not love," John pleads, "by word nor with the tongue; but in deed and truth." In my opinion, truth should be explained in terms of its meaning in the immediately following statement where the truth is a reference to the truth of the gospel (19a), as also in 2:21, Second John 2, 4, and Third John 3–4, 8. In that case, the relationship between the various terms can be defined as follows: The first two terms are related as the second pair are related; word and tongue, on the one hand, since words are produced by means of the tongue; deed and truth, on the other, deed referring to the deeds which derive from the truth of the gospel, the truth which produces the deeds as the tongue produces words. So the exhortation is to a practice of love within the sphere of actual work to which one is moved by the truth of the gospel, as opposed to love that deals only in empty words, perhaps similar to the good wishes James mentions (in 2:15–16).

"In this," John continues in verse 19, "shall we know that we are of the truth, ..." Again we have the debate over whether "in this" refers to what precedes or to what follows. On the ground that there is nothing in what follows that provides evidence "that we are of the truth," I hold that the reference is to what precedes. *In this*, then, refers to the practice of such love as has been defined in verse 18. By means of the practice of such love "we shall know that we derive from[38] or belong to the truth"—i. e., our spiritual existence derives from the truth of the gospel, which is to say that we derive from God (2:29; 3:10; cf. 4:1, 2, 3, 4, 6), rather than from the devil (3:8, 10, 12) who is "a liar and the father thereof" (John 8:44). This explanation is consistent with what John has said about love of the brothers being evidence of life (14).

The genuine practice of love of the brothers not only gives evidence "that we are of the truth," but in addition, as a consequence of this knowledge, provides peace for a troubled conscience, laying any doubts to rest (19b–20). "In this," referring to practice of genuine love of the brothers, "we shall know that we are of the truth," but in addition, knowing that we are of the truth, "we shall persuade our heart before him" (19b). The primary meaning of the Greek *peitho* is to persuade, and I see no reason for departing from the usual sense, though many have suggested alternate translations because of the difficulty of making the connection with verse 20. Arndt and Gingrich, for example, think the meaning here is "conciliate, pacify, set at ease or rest" (AG, 639).

Each of the clauses of verse 20 begin with *hoti*, which can mean either *that* or *because*. The experts have experimented with the two meanings in an effort to determine which best fits, whether one or the other, or one in one clause and the other in the other clause.

I opt for *that* in both clauses. Thus the first one will read: *that if our heart condemn us*, etc. This clause indicates the circumstances in which our heart needs to be persuaded. The word for condemn is *kataginosko*: to know against, condemn or convict; hence, "to find fault with, blame," perhaps "to accuse, condemn" (GT, 330; cf. AG, 409). Compare First Cor. 4:4 for the idea, though not the word: "I know nothing against myself." The word heart is used in the same sense as at First Sam. 24:5 where we read that "David's heart smote him." The reference is clearly to the conscience. So the question being discussed is how we may find rest or peace for our heart when our heart (i. e., conscience) knows something against or accuses us.[39]

---

[38] Grk *ek*, out of.

[39] Some secure the same result with regard to this clause by treating the *hoti* as the neuter of *hostis*, and rendering it "whenever" or the like. Thus: "whereinsoever our heart condemn us" (ASV margin); "in whatever our heart condemns us" (NASB); "whenever our hearts condemn us" (RSV & NRSV).

Translate *that* in the second clause as well: *that God is greater than our heart, and knows all things.* This clause is the object of the persuasion of heart. We persuade our heart, if it accuses us, that God is greater than our heart and knows everything. What is it about this superior knowledge of God that puts our heart at rest when it accuses us? Go back to the "in this" or "hereby" clause in 19. By practicing genuine love of the brothers "we shall know that we are of the truth." Furthermore, "we know that we have passed out of death into life, because we love the brothers" (14). How do we know that? We know it because God has told us. We may not be sinless, and our heart may accuse us. But God, who "is greater than our heart and knows everything," has assured us that if we are practicing love of the brothers "we are of the truth" and "we have passed out of death into life." With his superior knowledge, he knows that love of the brothers is evidence of our spiritual state, despite the misgivings of our heart. So we need to listen to God and not to our heart. He knows more than our heart knows about the evidence of spiritual status.[40]

True, some have interpreted verse 20 otherwise: If our heart condemns us, we may be sure that God, who knows even more than our heart, will condemn us even more. But surely that view runs contrary to the entire context, in which the emphasis is on assurance and the evidence of a right relationship with God.[41]

Fruit of an Uncondemning Heart (21–22)

First the condition: "if our heart condemn us not"—i. e., if it does not accuse us, or smite us, as David's heart did (1 Sam. 24:5), appar-

---

[40] The argument here is similar to Romans 8:31–34. "If God is for us, who is against us? ... Who shall lay anything to the charge of God's elect? It is God that justifies; who is he that condemns?" The superiority of God to any who may stand against his elect is an essential element in this reasoning. So also in First John 3:19–20, where the argument is that if God, with his superior knowledge of all the circumstances and his understanding of the significance of love for the brothers, does not condemn us, then neither should our own heart. "God is greater than our heart," and understands things which our heart does not.

[41] "The aim of the whole passage is surely to give assurance, and not to strike terror into their hearts" (Brooke).

ently on the ground that we understand the truth taught in verses 19–20. We know that we love the brothers; we are treating our brothers the way we were taught; and we take God's word for the evidence that provides with regard to our spiritual status, on which ground the accusations of the heart have been silenced. What then follows? The fruit of the uncondemning heart is twofold:

First, "we have boldness toward God" (21). This word was first used (in 2:28) for boldness in the presence of the Lord at his coming (or presence). But here the original emphasis on freedom of speech is certainly retained, for verse 20 indicates that John has in mind the boldness we have when we approach God in prayer.

Second, answered prayer: "and whatever we ask we receive of him, because we keep his commandments and do the things that are pleasing in his sight" (22). As in Chapter 2, the emphasis in the context is again on the commandments relating to the treatment of our brothers. See further below.

So the boldness to ask for great things is combined with an assurance that we receive "whatever we ask."

Boldness in prayer comes up again at First John 5:14. "And this is the boldness which we have toward him, that, if we ask anything according to his will, he hears us: ..."

The reason we receive what we ask is that the petition comes from one in tune with divine will and purpose, one who does not wish for that which would be contrary to the will of God. Jesus taught his disciples to pray with regard to the honor and glory of God before asking anything for self, in other words, to seek the kingdom first in our praying (Matt. 6:9–10 with v. 33). Thus we are to seek the will of God before anything else, and that determines the way we ask for ourselves. Prayer becomes a matter of seeking the will of God; a means of carrying on a relationship with God; a means of growth, of fine tuning a spiritual mind.

The Commandment Explained (23)

After relating a Christian's success in prayer to the fact that "we keep his commandments and [which is the same thing] do the things that are pleasing in his sight," John explains "his commandments." But again (as in 2:3–11), "his commandments" are summed up as a single commandment, which, however, is twofold. It has two related aspects: "And this is his commandment, that we should believe the name of his Son Jesus Christ, and love one another, even as he gave us commandment."

In the previous passage, the single commandment which summarized all the commandments was the commandment: "love one another." Here John adds an essential element of the command to love one another, without which this command could neither be understood nor obeyed: "that we should believe the name of his Son Jesus Christ." It is not "believe in (or on) the name," but literally "believe the name."[42] We should consult the lexicons (GT, 447; AG, 570) for this usage of *the name* (Grk *onoma*). Thus GT has the following explanation: "By a usage chiefly Hebraistic the *name* is used for everything which the name covers, everything the thought or feeling of which is roused in the mind by mentioning, hearing, remembering, the name, i. e. for *one's rank, authority, interests, pleasure, command, excellences, deeds,* etc."[43]

So *the name of his Son Jesus Christ* is who he is. It stands for all that he is; all that he has been revealed to be. *Belief in his name* is acceptance of all that he has been shown to be. We are called upon to confess "that Jesus is the Christ" (2:22; cf. 5:1); "that Jesus Christ is come in the flesh" (4:2); "that Jesus is the Son of God" (4:15; cf. 5:5).

The commandment to believe the name of his Son Jesus Christ has not appeared in First John until now, although we have had 2:22–24 with regard to the confession of the Son. But it is plain to see that belief in the name of the Son Jesus Christ is an essential precondition to loving one's brothers. Love is defined for Christians by its manifestation at the cross (3:16; 4:9–10). The love of God is manifested in the sending of his Son as the propitiation for our sins (4:10). This love reaches its end in us when we love each other (2:5; 4:12). "We love because he first loved us" (4:19). But if Jesus was not the Son of God, then the cross ceases to be such a great manifestation of the love of God. If we do not believe that Jesus was all that he has been revealed to be, then the cross cannot be viewed as the great manifestation of the love of God and the thing that moves us to love each other with that same sort of love does not exist. Therefore, belief in the name of God's

---

[42] In 5:13, however, it is *eis the name*.

[43] See further for examples.

Son Jesus Christ is essential to the love God wants us to have for each other. So *the commandment* (in 3:23) is not actually two commandments, but one, with two closely connected elements.

Assurance with Regard to the Relationship with God Grounded on the Keeping of the Commandments (24)

Finally John sets forth the keeping of the commandments as evidence of the right relationship with God: "And he that keeps his commandments remains in him, and he in him. And in this we know that he remains in us, ..." (24). Now we have a return to the plural "commandments," but in this context, in which love of the brothers has been set forth as evidence of our spiritual status (14, 19), the plural would again (as in 2:4–6) seem to have special reference to all the commandments that can be summarized in the one commandment to love one another; in other words, all the commandments that relate to how we are to treat each other.

So the essential point with regard to the assurance of spiritual status and relationship with God is not new (for see 2:3–11). But one point is added, and the addition is closely related to the argument John has developed in this context (19–20). The addition answers the question: How do we know that the one who loves his brothers, this love being shown by his behavior toward them, has this fellowship with God? The answer is: "We know ... from the Spirit which he gave us." I have preferred to translate "from" instead of "by" because the Greek preposition is *ek*, which means "out of." John is speaking of the source of our knowledge. We know that the one who loves his brother has fellowship with God because the Spirit God gave us has told us so. This last clause, therefore, lends confirmation to the reasoning in verses 19–20. By the love which we practice toward our brothers "we know that we are of the truth," and we know it despite the accusations of our conscience, which are silenced by our understanding "that God is greater than our heart, and knows all things" and he has assured us through the teaching of his Spirit that love of the brothers is certain evidence of our spiritual standing with him.

To be sure, verse 24 does not in itself say that we know these things through the teaching of the Spirit. It only says that the Spirit God gave us is the source of our knowledge. But the very next verse (4:1) will show that the way the Spirit is manifested among the children of God is through the presence of prophets in their midst, which is to say, spokesmen for God, men who spoke for God by revelation of the Spirit. Furthermore, the point will be confirmed when John returns to the subject at 4:12–15. At that place the gift of the Spirit (13) is connected with the testimony of the apostolic witnesses (14). Anyone who responds to that testimony by confessing "that Jesus is the Son of God" has assurance that he is in fellowship with God (15). It is by revelation of the Spirit that we understand the meaning of the cross (10). The same point is found in Romans 5:5.

So the evidence of our relationship with God that derives from the Spirit is not some "better felt than told" feeling or some inward voice, which would need to be tested for agreement with the testimony of the apostles (4:1–6), but is based on the revelation of the Spirit, which was manifested in the first century through the presence of prophets in the church and now is preserved in the apostolic writings found in the New Testament. Then the Word was in men; now it is preserved in these writings.

FIRST JOHN 4:1–6
Testing the Spirits: How to Tell the Difference Between the Spirit of Truth and the Spirit of Error

It seems plausible to relate Chapter 4 to 3:23, as Findlay does. That is the verse where John summarized the commandments as a single commandment with two closely connected aspects: "And this is his commandment, that we should believe the name of his Son Jesus Christ, and love one another, even as he gave us commandment." The first subdivision of Chapter 4 (4:1–6) deals with the first, belief in the name of God's Son; the second (4:7–21) elaborates the command to love one another.

But the first part (4:1–6) has a more immediate connection with the very last sentence of Chapter 3: "And in this we know that he remains in us, from[44] the Spirit which he gave us." The certainty that the one who keeps the commandments is in the right relationship with God derives from the Spirit's own revelation to us. But we must be certain that the Spirit we listen to is the one God gave. So the fourth chapter begins with a word of caution.

The Need to be Discriminating with Regard to the Spirits (1)

Again (as in 3:2 & 21 and then later in 4:7 & 11) John addresses his readers as "Beloved." They are his spiritual children (4:4) and he cares deeply for them. He does not want them to be deceived and led astray (cf. 2:26; 3:7) by the liars (2:22) and deceivers who have arisen (2:18) with new teaching that is different from that which they had received from apostolic witnesses in the beginning (2:24).

Certainty concerning the relationship with God derives from the Spirit he gave us, John has said (3:24b). But not every spirit can be believed. John exhorts his readers: "prove the spirits, whether they are from[45] God." Then he cites the reason[46] such testing is necessary: "because many false prophets are gone out into the world."

So we see that the plural "spirits" refers to manifestations of a spirit through prophets. *False prophets* are men who speak falsehoods under

---

[44] Grk *ek*, out of.
[45] Again the Greek *ek*.
[46] Grk *hoti*.

the cover of being inspired spokesmen for God.[47] Consult also First Cor. 14:12, 32, where "spirits" refers to spiritual gifts, various manifestations of the spirit. The second of these verses refers specifically to "the spirits of the prophets."

The Greek *dokimazo* means to put a thing to the test in order to determine whether it is genuine or not (GT, 154; AG, 202). It is used, for example, in the Greek Old Testament (Prov. 8:10; 17:3; Zech. 13:9) and also in the New Testament (1 Pet. 1:7; cf. 1 Cor. 3:12–13) in comparisons to the testing of precious metals. Today various devices are used in the printing of money so that it may be tested and one may be able to determine whether it is genuine or counterfeit. But how can the spirits be proved?

The Test to be Applied: What They Say About Jesus (2–3)

The test is not based on what they claim or how they feel. We are not called upon to do the impossible and look into a man's heart. The test is based on teaching, and specifically, what the prophet says about Jesus: "In this know you[48] the Spirit of God: every spirit who confesses Jesus Christ having come[49] in the flesh is from[50] God."[51]

On the other hand, "every spirit that does not confess Jesus is not from God." On the contrary, this spirit "is that which belongs to the antichrist, of which you have heard that it comes, and now it is in the world already" (cf. 2:18). Again, the antichrist does not appear to be a single individual. The term is used collectively, and the coming of

---

[47] See AG, 892 & GT, 676 on *pseudoprophetes*.

[48] The translation takes the verb as imperative rather than indicative.

[49] Greek perfect tense refers to something done in the past that continues to have its effect in the present.

[50] Grk *ek*.

[51] It is true, of course, that false prophets may come in sheep's clothing, professing a connection with Christ that is not genuine and true (Matt. 7:15–23), in which case Jesus assures his disciples that they may be recognized by their fruit: Are they doing the will of God or do they practice lawlessness? Do their lives indicate the obedience to Jesus which one owes to the person whose authority they acknowledge by calling him "Lord"? (Luke 6:46). First John 4:2–3 does not seem to take this complication into consideration. Perhaps John is setting forth a test that would be conclusive in the specific situation dealt with by his readers. The test assumes that the prophet is saying what he really believes about Jesus.

antichrist has been manifested by the appearance of a plurality of antichrists (2:18), or (as 4:1 puts it), the many false prophets who have gone out into the world, who deny "that Jesus is the Christ" (2:22).

The substance of the confession as expressed in 4:2–3, "Jesus Christ come in the flesh," may have special reference to views taken by John's opponents. When 5:6 is added to the discussion, it is apparent that these false prophets held views similar to those of Cerinthus, who taught that Christhood (or Sonship) was something that came on Jesus when he was baptized but departed from him before he died on the cross. The correct confession is an acknowledgment that in Jesus deity had been incarnated (John 1:1, 14).

Victory Over the Antichrist (4)

The pronoun at the beginning of verse 4 is expressed in Greek rather than being implied by the verb ending, which makes it emphatic: *You* in contrast to the spirit of the antichrist, of which John has said that it "is not of God." "*You* [in emphatic contrast to every spirit that does not confess Jesus, which is therefore not from God (v. 3) but from the world (v. 5)] are from God." Again the preposition is *ek*, out of, and indicates source or derivation.

You, John continues, "have overcome them." The false prophets had arisen, had asserted their position, and made their arguments, but John's little children had fought this spiritual battle and won.

An explanation of their victory is given in the second half of the verse: "because (Grk *hoti*) greater is he that is in you than he that is in the world" (4b). *He that is in you* is God, perhaps God in Christ. So John has said in 3:24. But he has also referred to the greatness of God: "God is greater than our heart, and knows all things" (3:20). This superior knowledge is probably to the point in 4:4b as well. The opponents of John's little children were false prophets, who had in them the spirit of antichrist. They did not have the spirit of truth (cf. 6b) in them. They were liars and deceivers, who were ignorant of the truth (cf. 2:22). But John's readers had the spirit of truth in them; they knew the truth (cf. 2:20–21). They had won the conflict by means of the power of the truth.

This explanation would seem to be justified by a previous passage in which John explains the medium by means of which God dwelt in his readers: "I have written unto you, young men, because you are strong, and the word of God remains in you, and you have overcome the evil one" (2:14b). The source of their strength was the word of God, which was in them, enabling them to overcome. Thus the medium by which their great God dwelt in them was the word of God, from which they derived strength to fight the battle and to win. Cf. also 2:24 & 27.

Contrast: The False Prophets and the Apostolic Witnesses (5–6)

Each of these verses also begins with an emphatic pronoun. In each case the pronoun is expressed rather than merely being implied by the verb ending.

First with regard to the false prophets: "They (emphatic contrast to *you* in verse 4) are from (Grk *ek* again) the world" (5a). They are not from God (3). They are from the world (5a). "For which reason (Grk *dia touto*)," John goes on to say, "they speak from (Grk *ek*) the world" (5b). The source of their speech is the world in its present state of alienation from God (cf. 5:19). They speak the language of the world, as some explain. Their speech derives from worldly thinking and worldly philosophy.

John adds: "and the world hears them." Their teaching is exactly what the world wants to hear.

Then the contrast: "We (again emphatic) are from (Grk *ek*) God" (6a). God is the one who has sent us. Our speech originates with God, who is its source.

Sometimes "we" in First John embraces the readers with the writer. Some argue for that view here. But I do not see how that is possible. For John goes on to say: "he that knows God hears us; he who is not from (Grk *ek*) God hears us not." If "we" includes all Christians, who in that case would be the one who knows God and hears "us"? Would the speaker and the hearer not be the same in that case? Is John guilty of such an absurdity as to say that Christians prove that they are of God by listening to themselves? No. Just as the world that hears the false prophets is distinguished from the speakers who derive from the world and speak the world's language, even so the one who knows God and hears "us" is distinguished from "we," the speakers who are from God.

The fact is, this is not a case in which "we" is set only in contrast to "they" (5), so that "we" means we Christians. The "we" is also in contrast to "you" (4). So "we" is a special group of Christians, which stands in contrast to the readers, who are also Christians.

We must go back to the prologue (1:1–4) in order to understand this "we" which stands in contrast to both "they" (the false prophets) and "you" (the readers). The reference is to John and his colleagues, the apostolic witnesses. The one who knows God listens to us; the one who is not from God does not listen to us.

Now John is ready to wrap up the discussion: "From (Grk *ek*) this we know the spirit of truth, and the spirit of error" (6b). John had started by calling upon his readers to prove the spirits (1). Now finally the test of the spirits (in the prophets) comes down to this: The one who is from God, who knows God, will pay attention to the apostolic witnesses; the one who is not of God will not hear them. The distinction between the false and the true finally comes down to whether a teacher gives attention to the testimony of Jesus' original witnesses.

After the three emphatic pronouns which stand at the beginning of verses 4, 5, and 6, now in 6b we have a case in which the pronoun is not emphatic. It is merely identified by the verb ending and is not expressed. The "we" in "we know" is not a special group of disciples, as in 6a, "we" in emphatic contrast not only to "they" (5) but also "you" (4), but embraces all Christians. Any Christian can apply the test John has laid down and identify and distinguish "the spirit of truth and the spirit of error."

Does verse 6 lay down a different test than the one given in verses 2 & 3? No. It is precisely the same. For verse 6 refers to the apostolic witnesses as men who knew firsthand and then spoke the truth about Jesus Christ. The teaching of all who come later (2–3) must be evaluated and judged for its agreement with the original witnesses (6). So, finally, this passage defines for us what was meant back in 2:24 by "that which you heard from the beginning." Reference is made to that which was first heard from one or more of the apostolic witnesses.

While we are at it we must take note that the author of the book mentioned in the preface comes to grief at this very point. His view is that Christianity must be revised in every age and adapted to new learning. But one of Jesus' original witnesses has told us that the distinction between the true teacher and the false lies in whether the teacher listens to the apostolic witnesses appointed by Christ. Clearly this author is moved by the spirit of antichrist. He is not of Christ or of God. Whatever name he wants to attach to his religion, it is plainly not Christianity.

FIRST JOHN 4:7–5:4

Love of the Brothers and Confession of Christ, the Combination Brought into Relation, as Manifesting the Relation to God

As we come to the second distinct passage of Chapter 4 we should recall the connection with 3:23, the twosided commandment. The first aspect, belief in the name of the Son, was discussed in 4:1–6. In fact, it is the second passage dealing with the identity of Jesus Christ and acknowledgment of the truth about him. The other is 2:18–27.

Now John turns to the other side of the commandment, love of the brothers. Love of the brothers as evidence of the relationship with God had also been the subject of earlier passages, 2:7–11 & 3:13–24.

In the present passage the two topics are shown to be connected. In fact they are so closely intertwined that they cannot be separated. Thus belief in the name of the Son and love of the brothers are a single commandment with two aspects (as already implied by 3:23).

I have extended the present unit to 5:4, rather than ending at 4:21. The reason is that 5:1–4 continues the discussion of the two topics, love of the brothers and faith in Jesus Christ, in relation to each other.

Exhortation to "Love One Another," Supported by Reference to the Character and Nature of God (7–11)

The return to the commandment (3:23) takes the form of an exhortation: "let us love one another" (7a). It is addressed to those whom John regards as "beloved." It is plain throughout that the whole epistle grows out of the regard which John has for his spiritual children. A reason is then given why Christians should love one another: "because[52] love is from[53] God," and furthermore, a person's relationship with God is manifested by love: "and every one that loves is begotten from[54] God, and knows God" (7b). Plainly John is not referring to just any emotion which some person wants to dignify by the name love. Love has been defined already (in 3:16–18) and will be further defined and explained in the following context.

---

[52] Grk *hoti*, because.

[53] Grk preposition *ek*, out of. Love derives from God; it has its origin or source in God.

[54] Again the preposition is *ek*.

72

The converse is also true: "He that does not love does not know God," and the reason is given: "because[55] God is love." Love is of the nature and essence of God. John does not say, "Love is God," so that one may conjure up some definition of love and then decide that that is what God is like. One cannot start with love. He must start with God. It is the character of God that defines what love is, and not the other way around.

Love has been defined historically by the manifestation of God in Christ (9–10): "In this the love of God was manifested in us,[56] that God has sent his only begotten Son into the world that we might live through him. In this is love, not that we loved God, but that he loved us, and sent his Son as the propitiation for our sins." In both these cases "in this" is explained by the following prepositional clauses.[57]

Can anyone look at the cross and doubt that the essential character of God is love? Again we see that love is not defined by an act of man, but by the act of God.[58] So again we have reason to make the point that one does not look first to love as practiced among men, and conclude that we know something about God from what we have found among men. Rather, one must look first to God to learn about love as it ought to be practiced among men.

Such a manifestation of God's love brings us under obligation ("ought," Grk *opheilo*) to love one another: "Beloved, if God so[59] loved us, we also ought to love one another" (11).

John's "break points" are difficult to make out, but the conclusion in verse 11 seems to complete the development of thought begun at 7a.

Certainty with Regard to Fellowship with God Through Revelation of the Spirit (12–16)

As the first subdivision was defined by the way it begins and ends (7 & 11), so also the second (12 & 16). As the first began with an assertion

---

[55] Grk *hoti*.

[56] Perhaps *in our case*.

[57] But in some cases no such defining clause follows, and the reference of "in this" must be sought in what precedes.

[58] See the note on 2:2 for discussion of the word "propitiation."

[59] The Greek *houtos* is an adverb of manner: in this way, in this manner, here: in the manner just described; contextually denoting degree. See GT, 468 & AG, 597. We are reminded of the "so" in John 3:16, where *houtos* is very emphatic, standing first in the sentence as it does.

about God (7b), so the new development begins with another assertion about God: "No man has beheld (or seen) God at any time" (12a; cf. John 1:18). But God is manifested in us "if we love one another," and John continues: "if we love one another, God remains in us, and his love is perfected (i. e., brought to its end or goal) in us" (12b). *God remains in us* in that his character is manifested in us. The perfecting of God's love in us was first mentioned at 2:5a. The Greek verb is again *teleioo* which means to bring to an end (*telos*). Consult First Timothy 1:5 and First Peter 1:9 for *telos* in the sense of purpose, aim or object. The purpose, aim or object of the love of God manifested at the cross was to reproduce itself in us. The love which is the essence of God's character (7–8), which was manifested by the cross (9–10), reaches its end or goal when we practice that kind of love toward one another (cf. 3:16–18). Thus God is in us and his love reaches its end in us.

But how do we know that? "In this we know that we remain in him and he in us, because he has given us from[60] his Spirit" (13). This verse returns to the thought of 3:24, where the Spirit God gave is said to be the source of the knowledge that the one who practices love remains in God and God in him. But recall also the immediately following statement (4:1), which indicates that this information comes from the Spirit through prophets who spoke for God. So the point is that this knowledge of who is in fellowship with God comes by revelation of the Spirit. The Spirit has explained everything we need to know.

Pay precise attention to what is said here. In the first reference to the Spirit back in 3:24b John had said God gave us the Spirit. The knowledge we have derives *from the Spirit which he gave us.* But in 4:13 John does not say God has given us his Spirit, but he has given us *from* his Spirit. So again (as in 3:24b) the emphasis is upon something that has been given from the Spirit which he gave us. The thing derived from the Spirit God gave is the same in each of these verses. John is explaining how we know who is in fellowship with God (we in him, he in us). "We know ... from the Spirit which he gave us" (3:24b). "We know ... because he has given us from his Spirit." The thing we have from the Spirit is knowledge, which is something that derives from revelation of the Spirit, and that comes through God's appointed spokesmen (as 4:1 proves).[61]

---

[60] Grk *ek*, literally *out of*, hence *from*, indicating source.

[61] Confirmation of this point is also found in the parallel between 2:14b and
footnote continued on next page

Verse 14 is consistent with this explanation about how the Spirit communicates this certainty, namely, that it is not a matter of some "better felt than told" inward feeling within each Christian, but rather a matter of divine revelation of the Spirit through God's appointed spokesmen: "And we have beheld (or seen) and bear witness that the Father hath sent the Son as the Savior of the world." The "we" is emphatic as the pronouns were emphatic in verses 4–6a. (The pronoun is expressed in Greek and not just indicated by the verb ending.) And just as the "we" in 6a had special reference to the apostolic witnesses, so also the "we" in verse 14. "We" cannot embrace all the Christians. Not all Christians "have beheld and bear witness that the Father has sent the Son as the Savior of the world" any more than it is true that any man "beheld" God (12a). This language refers to the apostolic witnesses, just as the same language did in 1:1–4, where the writer speaks of himself and his colleagues, the other apostles, as seeing, beholding, and then bearing witness, declaring, and even writing about the things they had seen and heard, so that the readers might have fellowship with them, which was a fellowship with the Father and the Son.

Observe the way the testimony of the Spirit and the testimony of the apostles are combined in John 15:26–27, just as they are in First John 4:13–14. The Holy Spirit, said Jesus, "shall bear witness of me, and you also bear witness, because you have been with me from the beginning." Thus the apostles saw and could bear witness that the Father has sent the Son as the Savior of the world. But that language does not apply to Christians who have not been with Jesus from the beginning. We have not seen what the apostles saw. We cannot testify to what we have seen as they did.

Two things were necessary to qualify the apostles as witnesses of Christ. First, they had to experience the events. Second, the Spirit had to come upon them. They could have told what they saw and heard

---

4:4. The second of these verses attribute the readers' victory over the antichrists to the fact that the one in them is greater than the one in the world. God was in them, and the greatness spoken of relates specifically to knowledge (as in 3:20). It is knowledge of the truth, which comes to us by divine revelation. The parallel in 2:14b proves as much. In that verse victory over the evil one is attributed to strength which comes from the word of God which is in the persons addressed. God is in them through the word of God which is in them, and the power of truth is greater than that of the error taught by antichrists.

even before the Spirit came. Yet Jesus wanted them to wait for the coming of the Spirit before giving their testimony (Luke 24:48–49; Acts 1:1–5, 8). The reason is that the Holy Spirit would explain the meaning of what they had seen. They could have told what they saw about the crucifixion and the resurrection. But they would not have understood the meaning of the cross without revelation from the Spirit.

This explanation must also be borne in mind in the consideration of the statement at Romans 5:5 which closely parallels the present passage. "... The love of God has been poured out in our hearts through the Holy Spirit which was given to us." It was the revelation of the Holy Spirit that explained the meaning of the cross (cf. Rom. 5:6–8).

So also in First John 4:12–14. It is revelation of the Spirit through the witnesses that enables us to understand that God is in us when we love each other. But John is not done.

The subject of the sentence in 4:14 is an emphatic "we," referring to the apostolic witnesses (as in 1:1–4). This "we" does not embrace every Christian. Not everyone has seen and therefore not everyone can bear witness. But anyone can have the fellowship with God possessed by the apostles through the revelation made to them: "Whoever shall confess that Jesus is the Son of God, God remains in him and he in God" (15).

Confession is an expression of one's belief, belief in "the name of his Son Jesus Christ" (3:23; cf. 5:13), belief "that Jesus is the Christ" (5:1), belief "that Jesus is the Son of God" (5:5). And the confession that Jesus is the Son of God is based on the testimony of the witnesses (4:14); it is a response to the evidence presented by the apostles. "Belief arises from the thing heard,[63] and the thing heard comes through the word of Christ"[64] Recall that Jesus' prayer was first for his chosen apostles and then "for them that believe on me through their word" (John 17:20).

"Whoever" is consistent with the way John deals with everything as black and white, with no gray areas—light and darkness, truth versus the lie, love and hate. He does not deal with the complication that someone may confess what he does not really believe or that his conduct may not

---

[63] The same Greek as for "report" in verse 16.

[64] An attempt at a literal translation of Romans 10:17, with the words *arises* and *comes* supplied. The manuscripts differ over whether the reading should be *the word of Christ* or *the word of God*. Each of the two readings has strong textual support in the manuscripts.

be consistent with his profession. Other passages do deal with such complications (1:6, 2:4, 9; cf. Matt. 7:15–23; 2 Cor. 11:13–15), but here, presumably, the confession is understood as representing what one really believes and the confessor is understood as living out the implications of his confession. So the same assurance is given those who confess that Jesus is the Son of God (4:15) that was given those who love their fellow Christians (4:12–13). The two are one. None do one but not the other. The next verse assumes this connectedness.

John continues: "And we have known and have believed[65] the love which God has in us (or in our case)" (16). John refers to the love which was manifested at the cross (8–10). In point of fact, this manifestation of God's love was "for the whole world" (2:2; cf. John 3:16). But not everyone in the world has confessed that Jesus is the Son of God (15), and those who do not acknowledge the identity of Jesus cannot understand and put their trust in that great manifestation of God's love which took place at the cross.

That may explain why the "we" in 16a is emphatic, even though the reference is to the experience of all Christians and not just to a certain group of Christians (i. e., the apostolic witnesses). Whoever confesses that Jesus is the son of God has fellowship with God (15). And in fact "we" have made that confession, and consequently know and believe that love. "We" does not stand in contrast to other Christians, but in contrast with nonconfessors.

One who does not believe and confess that Jesus is the Son of God cannot understand what happened at the cross. If Jesus was not the Son of God, then the cross is not the great manifestation of divine love John has made it out to be (8–10).

Now John is ready to repeat the assertion about the essential character and nature of God first made in verse 8, and then to wrap up and conclude the development of thought beginning at verse 12: "God is love; and he that remains in love remains in God, and God remains in him" (16b).

---

[65] Both verbs are in the perfect tense, which refers to an act that takes place in the past but continues to have its effect in the present. The verbs reach back to the past when John and his readers came to know and to believe the meaning of the cross, the point of conviction and conversion, in other words. But this knowledge and belief continues to be effective to the present time.

Nothing new is found here except the description *he that remains in love*, and even that is defined by an alternative expression found at the beginning of the subsection 4:12–16. Consequently every term must be explained in light of the preceding context. *God is love.* So John had said at the beginning (8), immediately proving his point about the essential character of God by reference to the manifestation of God's love in the sacrifice of his only begotten Son (9–10). *He that remains in love* is substituted for the condition laid down at the beginning *if we love one another* (12). The one who remains in love is the one who practices love toward his brothers. But love is not some undefined and perhaps indefinable abstraction. Nor is it whatever a person wants to call love. The word is preceded by the Greek article in the clause *he that remains in love*, actually *the love*. It is that love which is defined by the character of God (4:8, 16), which was manifested by the sacrifice of the Son of God on the cross (4:9–10). It is love as thus defined that is to be practiced toward our brothers (3:16–18). We are to love each other as Christ Jesus loved us (John 13:34–35; 15:12–13); "to walk even as he walked" (1 John 2:6). It is that love which was manifested at the cross that is to be practiced among the disciples of Jesus. Thus the love of God will be in us (cf. 3:16–17). With all of this material behind us by the time we reach this section it comes as no surprise to find John saying: *he that remains in love remains in God, and God remains in him.* A person proves that it is so by practicing the same unselfish and even self-sacrificing love that is of the essence of God's character.

But one other point in this subsection remains to be developed. John had said: "If we love one another ... God's love is perfected in us" (12b). It is this concept of God's love being perfected (reaching its end, object, goal) in us that receives further development in the last section of Chapter 4. As was true of other aspects of the subject, this one too must be explained in the light of previous references to it.

Love Made Perfect: Divine Love Reaching Its End in Us (17–19)

The section begins with another of John's "In this" clauses: "In this is love made perfect with us, ..." (17a). Again (as in 3:10 & 19) "this" must be defined by what precedes. This view is much more likely than that "this" is defined by one of the following clauses. Brown points out the problem of connecting "this" with the next clause, "that[65] we may have boldness in the day of judgment" (17b): "The main difficulty centers on the awkward logic: love has reached perfection in something that has not yet happened."

The logic of connecting "this" with 17c, "because[66] as he is, even so are we in this world" is not as awkward. The connection would make better sense, in fact, not very different sense from the proposal I am making about the connection; and furthermore, the "in this" clauses are most often interpreted by a *hoti* clause. But this connection would make 17b parenthetical, which would be a pretty harsh construction. Westcott even calls it "unnatural." If this connection were intended by the author, he could have, should have, and probably would have reversed the order of 17b and 17c (Brown).

So we must look back to 16b for the explanation of "in this," so that "this" refers to the relationship with God that exists on the part of the one who remains in love. The thought agrees precisely with what was already said in 12b. *Love* (17a) is preceded by the article in the Greek. John is not referring to love as an abstract and undefined quality, but is referring specifically to that love which is from God (7a), which is defined by the character of God (8) and which was manifested by the sacrifice of God's only begotten Son (9–10). John has already said (in 12b) that when we love one another God's love is perfected (reaches its end, object or goal) in us. Now (at 17a) he picks up this same thought of the love of God reaching its end in us when we remain in love, and then carries the idea further by pointing out a consequence (or purpose) of God's love being perfected in us. *With us*, rather than *in us* (12b), means something like in cooperation with us (Westcott).[67]

The clause (17a) does not describe a flawless practice of love on our part. It speaks of the way the love of God (*the love* with the Greek article) attains its goal in us when we love one another, as in 12b. But here John adds a purpose clause: *in order that we may have boldness in the day of judgment.* The idea of *boldness ... be-*

---

[65] Grk *hina*.

[66] Grk *hoti*.

[67] Compare the similar usage in Acts 15:4. "They rehearsed all things that God had done with them."

fore him at his coming was introduced already at 2:28.[68] There boldness stood in contrast to shame. Here it is in contrast to fear (18). When we love each other the love of God manifested at the cross has attained its purpose with us and enables us to have boldness in the day of judgment.

The reason we are able to have such boldness is explained in 17c: "because as he is, even so are we in this world." *He*, literally *that one*, is Christ. We love as he loved (John 13:34; 15:12); we walk as he walked (1 John 2:6).[69] For that reason, that is, because of this consistency and harmony between us and God, we need have no fear of punishment, but can face the day of judgment with boldness.

John continues his discussion of this love made perfect in verse 18: "Fear is not in the love" (18a, lit. tr.).[70] Again love is preceded by the Greek article, and again John is not discussing love as an abstract concept, but refers specifically to love as defined in previous verses.

"But,"[71] he continues, "the perfect love casts out the fear, because the fear has punishment; but[72] the one who fears is not made perfect in the love" (18bc).

Again we must appeal to preceding context for the explanation of *the perfect love.* John is not speaking of the flawless practice of love on the part of Christians. Throughout the context to this point, when he has used the word perfect in connection with love, he has been speaking of the love of God manifested at the cross reaching its end or attaining its goal when it reproduces itself in us, i. e., when we love one another. God's love is perfected in us when we love one another (12). The perfect love must be explained as referring to the

---

[68] The Greek for boldness is *parresia*, which is discussed at 2:28 & 3:21. It appears once more at 5:14.

[69] See also verse 12 for the idea that the invisible God is manifested in those who love one another. Verse 16b also relates to the idea to some extent.

[70] Consider whether fear should be understood in an objective sense, the object of fear, the thing that causes fear (as in Rom. 13:3; 1 Pet. 3:14), the punishment. Nothing that causes fear is in this love. For this sense of *phobos*, study GT, 656 and AG, 863.

[71] The strong adversative *alla*.

[72] Grk *de*, indicating contrast.

love of God perfected in us when we love one another. If we must wait for the perfect practice of love on the part of human beings to cast out the fear, frankly we are going to be dealing with a lot of fear. No, the point is that the love of God, having reached its end in us when we love one another, does away with the fear—anything that would cause fear (cf. 1 Pet. 3:14).

A reason is given: "because the fear has punishment." God's love does not have punishment once it produces its fruit in us. It is fear that is associated with punishment. It possesses punishment. But once God's love has been perfected in us, the fear is driven out and with it the punishment that is associated with fear.

John has spoken of how the love of God is made perfect (or reaches its end) in us when we love one another. But finally *we* are made perfect in love when the love of God has done its work and reached its end by reproducing itself in us. On the other hand, the one who fears has not been made perfect in love (18c). He demonstrates that God's love has not yet done its work in him and reached its end in him, and he has not been brought to his own end in love. Otherwise the fear would be gone.

But when are we made perfect in love? It is when God's love has done its work and reached its end (object, goal) by reproducing itself in us. Thus love for the brothers is the end (object, goal) of God's love: "We love because he first loved us" (19). Our love derives from God's love (cf. 7, 11). It is natural to reciprocate the love which has done so much for us. But John is not speaking merely of this natural reciprocation of love toward God, who loved us so much. The love that we manifest is a love toward our brothers as well as toward God.

False Claim Refuted: The Impossibility of Loving God While Hating One's Brother (4:20–5:1)

In fact John goes so far as to say that one who claims to love God and at the same time hates his brother is a liar (20a). John does not say he is self-deceived, but that he is a liar. His claim is false.

This assertion (20a) is supported by an explanation introduced by the conjunction *gar*, "for" at the beginning of 20b. "for he that does not love his brother whom he has seen, cannot love God whom he has not seen" (20b). It is simply impossible that one could love God and not love his brother. The impossibility is related to the fact that the brother is seen, while God is not seen. Recall verse 12 for the idea that God is unseen, but manifested in those who love one another.

Several passages in the Gospel of John seem to be grounded on the same logic. Compare, for example, John 5:42–43 where the Jews are said to show that they do not love God by rejecting one who comes as representative of God.

Jesus told his brothers: "The world cannot hate you; ..." (7:7a). They belonged to the world. They were on friendly terms with the world. They did not challenge the deeds of the world.

Then again, Jesus tells the Jews: "If God were your Father, you would love me; for I came forth and am come from God; for neither have I come of myself, but he sent me" (John 8:42). Again the idea is that one shows his relation to God by his attitude toward a messenger who comes from God.

Again: "If you were of the world, the world would love its own: ..." (John 15:19).

The explanation of the assertion (in 20a) is continued in verse 21: "And this commandment have we from him, that he who loves God love his brother also." The love of God will soon be identified with keeping his commandments (5:2–3). Disobedience to the commandment from God to love one's brother provides further support for the assertion that one who claims to love God while hating his brother is a liar. He cannot claim to love God, for he does not obey God's command to love his brother.

We should not let the chapter division mislead us into thinking a totally new thought is being introduced at 5:1. The definition that is offered here continues to support the assertion that one who claims to love God while hating his brother is a liar (20a). When one understands this brotherhood of which John speaks, he will understand the impossibility of loving God while not loving his brother.

To the end of Chapter 4 John has spoken of loving one's brother. But just who is this brother whom we are commanded to love? Now (in 5:1) we are provided an explanation. John has been speaking of brothers in the family of God, those who are children of God as having been begotten of God: *Everyone who believes that Jesus is the Christ has been begotten from God: and everyone who loves the father who begets loves also the child that is begotten from him.* Once one fully realizes just who his brother really is, he will have no trouble understanding the assertion that he cannot love God without also loving the brother who has God's own seed planted within him and who therefore bears the nature of God (cf. 3:9).

82

Again (in 1a) it is important to pay attention to Greek tenses. The first verb is from a present participle;[73] hence everyone who is a believer at the present moment. *Has been begotten* is from a Greek perfect tense,[74] which refers to something that took place in the past, but continues to have its effect in the present; hence the translation. Everyone who believes now, at the present time, that Jesus is the Christ has been begotten of God at some point in the past and he continues to have this status as one begotten of God at the present moment. John is not at this place indicating how one becomes a child of God, but how one recognizes the brother (4:21) whom he is to love; he is presenting the present evidence that one is a child of God.

Now the concept set forth in 4:20 is as transparent as light. One who loves the father also loves the child who is begotten from that father, and therefore has something of that father in him. Once we grasp this point we will find it impossible even to imagine a love for God that does not also include love for our brothers who are the true children of God.

The Test: How We Know We Love the Children of God (5:2–3a)

Since the facts are such as have been presented in 4:20–5:1, i. e., if love of God is so essentially connected to love of one's brother, nothing could be more important to us than getting an answer to the question: Then just how do we know that we love the children of God?

"In this we know that we love the children of God, whenever we love God and do his commandments" (2). *In this* can only refer to what follows in this case, namely to the *whenever* clause.[75] Actually, if the words are taken literally, John is describing the point in time when we know that we love the children of God. It is at that point in time "when we love God and do his commandments."

Love for one's brother has been enjoined as a commandment in 4:21. But the plural "commandments" refers to the many acts in which love of one's brother is manifested (cf. Rom. 13:8–10). So the point should be clear. Love for one's brother is not proved by claims or by

---

[73] Grk *pisteuon.*

[74] Grk *geggenetai.*

[75] Grk *hotan* is "a particle of time, composed of *hote* and *an, at the time that, whenever*; used of things which one assumes will really occur, but the time of whose occurrence he does not definitely fix" (GT, 458); "temporal particle *at the time that, whenever, when* of an action that is conditional, possible, and, in many instances, repeated" (AG, 587).

inward feelings. It is behavior, how one acts as he obeys God's commandments with regard to proper treatment of a brother, that gives evidence that one loves his brother (cf. 3:16–18).

Verse 3a explains why the test is so stated, not merely "whenever we love God" but "whenever we love God and do his commandments": "For[76] this is the love of God, that we keep his commandments." Love for God is identified with the keeping of his commandments. One demonstrates love for God by keeping his commandments. But it is also the way one can be sure that he loves the children of God, for so many of God's commandments deal with behavior toward the children of God.

Characterization of God's Commandments (3b)

John adds a characterization of God's commandments: "and his commandments are not burdensome." The Greek *barus* means "heavy ... burdensome, difficult to fulfill" (AG, 134; cf. GT, 96). The scribes and the Pharisees, said Jesus, "bind heavy burdens (Grk *barea*) and grievous to be borne, and lay them on men's shoulders; but they themselves will not move them with their finger" (Matt. 23:4, ASV). Jesus, however, invites all who "labor and are heavy laden" to come and take his yoke upon them, with the assurance: "For my yoke is easy, and my burden is light" (Matt. 11:28–30).

This characterization of God's commandments is evidently added to assure the reader that the test John has proposed in verse 2 is one that can be met by those who love God. God's commandments are not heavy, a weighty burden, difficult if not impossible to carry. We can keep them.

Verse 4 then explains why God's commandments are not heavy.

The Reason God's Commandments Are Not Burdensome: Faith's Victory Over the World (4)

The explanation is introduced by the Greek *hoti* (because): "because whatever is begotten of God overcomes (or conquers) the world: and this is the victory that overcame[77] the world, our faith."

---

[76] Explanation introduced by the conjunction *gar*.

[77] Aorist participle, perhaps reflecting upon the victory over the world that becomes ours when we first become Christians.

After using the masculine (whoever) in verse 1, now John uses a neuter (whatever thing). Perhaps we cannot be sure of the reason. Is John thinking of the fetus that is brought into existence by the implanting of the divine seed (cf. Luke 1:35, "the holy thing that is begotten")? Is the intention to lay greater stress on universality?[78] I do not see a clue. We do find this unexpected neuter with reference to persons elsewhere in John's writing (e. g., John 3:6; 6:37, 39; 17:2, 7, 24). Blass and Debrunner in their scholarly *Greek Grammar* say the following: "The neuter is sometimes used with reference to persons if it is not the individuals but a generic quality that is to be emphasized."[79] In that case reference would seem to be not to the persons as such, but to something in that person or something about that person. But I am at a loss.

The world will be used in verse 19 for this present order under the rule of the evil one. It is the world with its lusts in conflict with the will of God, the love of which cannot coexist with the love of the Father (2:15–17). Its pull is opposed to the will of God and makes the divine commandments seem like a heavy burden to be born. It is listening to the spokesmen for the world, who spout the world's philosophy (4:5 in context of 1–6), that make God's commandments seem so heavy and burdensome and restrictive.[80]

---

[78] Or perhaps a collective aspect, the group of those begotten of God.

[79] Quoted in Brown, 541.

[80] So today. Without faith in Jesus Christ but adopting worldly relativism, parents do not expect their children to obey the commandments with regard to sexual morality. They see God's demand for sexual purity as much too heavy a burden for children to carry. So instead of teaching them to respect Biblical morality they teach them to "be careful" and to practice "safe" sex. It is the world and its philosophy that make the commandments seem heavy.

Even professing Christians apply worldly philosophy in marriage. "I cannot love and respect my mate any more," we may say, even though we entered into a sworn covenant before God, in which we promised to do so. This view that the commandments of God are too heavy to obey comes from worldly philosophy. The commandments will not seem so impossible to obey if we put our faith in Jesus Christ as Lord and King and simply trust and obey.

The commandments will be burdensome until the conquering power of faith in Jesus Christ liberates us from the power of the world and gives us victory.

Both of the latter passages speak of victory over the world. The young men among John's readers were strong because of the word of God in them and were able to overcome the evil one (2:14b). God was in the readers through the knowledge imparted to them by God's Spirit and had empowered them to overcome the world's teachers with their errors (4:4; cf. 3:20, 24). The seed of God planted in persons through the medium of God's Word provides the power for victory.

"And this is the conquering power[81] that conquered the world, our faith," the faith "that Jesus is the Christ" (1), "the Son of God" (5), the faith that gives evidence of one's being "begotten of God" (1) and thus a victor over the world (4a).

The aorist participle "has overcome (or conquered)" refers back to the initial victory over the world that became ours when we acknowledged Jesus as the Christ, the Son of God. At that point the victory over the world achieved by Christ Jesus (cf. John 16:33) became ours. Until then we were under the rule of the evil one (5:21), and under the power of the world, its lusts and all that is at odds with God (2:15–17); we listened to teachers who were of the world and who spoke the world's language and spouted the world's philosophy (4:5). But faith in Jesus Christ changed everything. The world no longer has such a hold on us. We have been delivered from that old bondage to the world. Now we "walk in the light" (1:7) and we can see things as they really are (2:8–11). We see the world and its lusts for what they really are. We see the false prophets who belong to the world, who speak of the world, to whom the world listens, for what they really are. And finally, we see the commandments of God in their true light, not as a burden too heavy to be lifted, but as a light and pleasant duty, a delight to perform. Thus verse 4 explains why "his commandments are not burdensome" (3b).

---

[81] "Conquering power" is from Raymond Brown, who describes the Greek *nike* as "a metonymy for the means of victory, or the power that grants victory." He makes reference to AG, 538: "victory, then as abstract for concrete the means for winning a victory (but cf. also the custom of speaking of the emperor's *nike* as the power that grants him the victory)."

═FIRST JOHN 5:5–12═
The Testimony to Jesus Christ

This epistle can seem like a seamless garment. The break points are often difficult to identify. Thus the first four verses of Chapter 5 have continued the development of the theme introduced in 4:7 without a perceptible break point. But finally, at 5:5 we find a statement that serves as a transition to a new theme which will then be discussed through 5:12. In this way verse 5 serves the same purpose as 1:5, 2:1, 7, 12, 18, 28–29, 3:13–14 and 4:1. In each case a new theme is introduced by linking into a concept found in the previous passage.

Thus verse 5 is transitional, moving from the assertion about the power of faith (4) to a more precise definition of that faith (5–6) followed by a statement of the grounds of it (7–12).

Precise Definition of the Believer Who Conquers the World (5–6)

John moves toward the new point with a question: "But who is the one that conquers[82] the world, but (or except) the one who believes that Jesus is the Son of God?" (5). None other! The expected answer to the rhetorical question is: Nobody! None other than the one who believes that Jesus is the Son of God conquers the world. He and he alone! Nobody can be named if not this one. The exceptive clause is introduced by the combination *ei me*, which is literally *if not*.[83] Who if not this one? So the idea is: Only this one.

But John's definition of the content of this world conquering faith goes further. Not only does this belief have as its object the proposition "that Jesus is the Son of God" (5), but the identity of this person is further defined: "This is the one who came[84] by means of[85] water and blood, Jesus Christ; not in the water only, but in the water and in the blood" (6).

---

[82] Present participle from *nikao*.

[83] See the discussion in GT, 171b.

[84] See First John 4:2 & Second John 7 for the coming of Christ.

[85] Grk *dia*.

Why would John be so emphatic about this point? Why would he be so insistent that the coming of Jesus Christ was *not in the water only, but in the water and in the blood*? I can see no other reason for this emphasis than that one or more of the teachers John was opposing must have held the view that the coming of Christ was in the water only and not also in the blood.

In fact a man named Certhinthus, of whom we know from Ignatius, held just such a view. He held that the heavenly Christ came upon the man Jesus when he was baptized, but then departed from him before he died on the cross. The consequence of this position, then, is that the person who died on the cross was not really the Son of God, but only the human Jesus. John seems to be opposing such a view, though not necessarily as held by the man Certhinthus, but someone holding a similar view. Thus the person who died on the cross was really God's only begotten Son, sent as the propitiation for our sins and sacrificed as a manifestation of the love of God (1 John 4:9–10). Thus the death of Jesus on the cross really was the sacrifice of God's only begotten Son and it really was the propitiation for our sins.[86]

Witness of the Spirit (7)[87]

But how do we know that John's assertions about the coming of Jesus are true? Evidence is presented beginning at verse 7: "And the

---

[86] "Only on John's view of it can the death of Jesus be the mighty act of God for our salvation. For John's opponents it was merely the human Jesus who died. All the force of John's statements that 'God showed his love to us' by sending his Son to die disappears if the One who died was not in fact Jesus Christ, the Son of God" (Marshall).

[87] The New KJV follows the same textual tradition as its predecessor in verses 7–8a: "For there are three who bear witness in heaven: the Father, the Word, and the Holy Spirit; and these three are one. And there are three that bear witness on earth: ..." But at least the revision has a marginal note in which the weakness of the textual evidence for this reading is indicated. An early printing of the New Testament contained the following note: "The words from 'in heaven' (v. 7) through 'on earth' (v. 8) are from the Latin Bible, although three Greek manuscripts from the 15th Century and later also contain them." The note was revised in a later printing to indicate that this reading is "found in

footnote continued on next page

Spirit is the one who bears witness,[88] because the Spirit is the truth." *The truth* is the truth about Christ Jesus (as in 2:21 & 3:19), which was revealed by the Holy Spirit. The Spirit is identified with the truth for precisely the same reason that Jesus himself claimed to be the truth.

Jesus had called himself the truth (John 14:6), the truth embodied in a person. As the revelation of deity the incarnate Word was "full of grace and truth" (John 1:14). "Grace and truth came through Jesus Christ" with a fulness that placed it in the sharpest contrast with any previous revelation (John 1:17); it was a revelation of God such as could only have come through God's only begotten Son (John 1:18). A new age had dawned with the coming of Christ, in which the Father would be worshipped in the light of this new revelation (John 4:23–24). Those who remained in the word of Jesus would be enlightened by soul liberating truth (John 8:31–32). Jesus was a man who spoke the truth which he heard from God (John 8:40; cf. vv. 45–46). He had come into the world in order to bear witness to the truth (John 18:37). He could, therefore, claim to be the truth (John 14:6), for the ultimate truth of divine revelation was embodied in himself.

But most people in the ancient world had not heard the truth directly from Jesus Christ. They encountered the truth as it came to them through spokesmen for God, apostles and prophets, who received their message by revelation of the Holy Spirit.[89] Thus John tells us: "And the Spirit is the one that bears witness," and then assigns as the reason: "because the Spirit is the truth."

Greek in only four or five very late manuscripts." Most, if not all, other versions omit the passage, not even judging it worthy of a place in the margin. See notes in the commentaries of Westcott, Brooke, Bruce, Marshall et al for discussion. I have chosen simply to refer to the version that includes it in the text, on the ground that the best that can be said for this reading is pretty damning. I appreciate the note indicating the paucity of the evidence for the reading. But God help the scholars who would put something into the text on the basis of such evidence. The reading smacks of something a copyist might have written in the margin, which was transferred to the text in later copies.

[88] Cf. RSV: "And the Spirit is the witness."

[89] Compare my exposition of Second Cor. 3:16–18 in *Thinking Through Second Corinthians*, 32f, note 27, in which that passage is explained along the same lines as I have proceeded in the exposition of the present text.

The Holy Spirit is identified with the truth for much the same reason as Jesus called himself the truth. The night before his death Jesus had fully explained the role of the Holy Spirit to his apostles in a private conversation which is recorded in John 13–16.

The first reference to the Holy Spirit is at John 14:16–18. "And I will make request of the Father, and he shall give you another helper (or counselor),[90] that he may be with you for ever, the Spirit of truth: ... I will not leave you orphans: I come to you."

"The Greek *paracletos* (helper, counselor) is literally one called alongside, especially as helper or lawyer, but later passages (14:25f; 15:26f; 16:7–15) define the way in which the Spirit assists the disciples. The Spirit of truth is called 'another Paraclete,' for Jesus himself has functioned in that role and the Spirit will function in his place once he has returned to the Father."[91]

Jesus assured his apostles, "I will not leave you orphans"[92] — one deprived of parents, but in this case referring to "those bereft of a teacher, guide, guardian" (GT, 454; cf. AG, 583). He had told them he would go away and, further, that they would not immediately be able to go where he was going (13:33–36), but that he would come again to take them to his Father's house (14:1–3). So his promise, "I come to you," added as a contrast to leaving them orphans, can only refer to the coming of the Holy Spirit, who would be sent in his name (14:26). It cannot refer to his personal coming to them after his resurrection from the dead, for in that case he would leave them orphans after all when he returned to heaven after forty days (cf. Acts 1:3).

Jesus begins to define the help the Holy Spirit would give them in the next passage: "These things have I spoken to you while remaining with you.[93] But the Paraclete, the Holy Spirit, whom the Father will send in my name, he shall teach you all things, and bring to your remembrance all that I said to you" (John 14:25–26).

---

[90] Greek *paracletos*.

[91] *Thinking Through John*, 109, n. 129.

[92] The Greek here is *orphanos*.

[93] Which shows that his words were addressed to a special group of disciples, the apostles, who had been with him from the beginning (cf. John 15:27; Acts

footnote continued on next page

In the next passage (John 15:26–27) the testimony of the Spirit is mentioned, just as in First John 5:7 the Spirit is said to be the one who testifies. As over against the false accusations of his opponents, Jesus speaks of the testimony by which he would be vindicated: "But when the Paraclete is come, whom I will send to you from the Father, the Spirit of truth, which proceeds from the Father, he shall bear witness of me; and you also bear witness because you have been with me from the beginning."

Observe the way the testimony of the Holy Spirit is linked to the human testimony of the apostles, just as it is in First John 4:13–14. Again it is plain that the promises are specially addressed to the apostles as men who had been with Jesus "from the beginning." No one today can claim to be a witness of Jesus in the sense that these men were witnesses of Jesus.

Then in John 16:7–11 Jesus again discussed the way the testimony of the Spirit would vindicate him and expose the error of the world about him (John 16:8–11); after which he added: "I have yet many things to say to you, but you cannot bear them now. Howbeit when he, the Spirit of truth, is come, he shall guide you into all the truth: ..." (John 16:12–13a). The promise is followed by an explanation of the truth that would be communicated to them through the Holy Spirit. It refers to the truth which the Spirit heard from God the Father.[94]

For the third time the Holy Spirit is referred to as "the Spirit of truth." He would guide the apostles "into all the truth." He would reveal to them the truth which came from the Father. So the Holy

---

1:21–22). These promises do not apply to all disciples through the ages. One strong illustration of the special application of these promises to the apostles is found in the assurance that the Holy Spirit would bring to their remembrance the things they had heard from Jesus. When Peter anticipated his own death (in Second Peter 1:12–16) he was concerned that the memory of the truth be preserved for his readers. He did not take the position that he need not be concerned about this problem, since the Lord had promised that the Spirit would bring the truth to remembrance. He saw the need to do something about it himself. What he did was to put the truth in writing, not only in two letters (2 Pet. 3:1–2) but also in the Gospel of Mark, which contains the memoirs of Peter put into writing by his assistant Mark.

[94] Paul makes the same point in First Cor. 2:6–13.

Spirit is identified with the truth in First John 5:7 for the same reason that Jesus himself had claimed to be the truth; and, in fact, John's
readers had heard the truth from the Holy Spirit through the apostles,
and not directly from Jesus himself. It is for that reason that for
them the Holy Spirit could be identified with the truth. They had
encountered the truth about Jesus not through personal contact with
Jesus in the manner of the apostles but through revelation of the
Holy Spirit. During Jesus' personal ministry people encountered
the truth as it was embodied in the person Jesus. But after Jesus'
ascension back to the Father people encountered the truth as it was
manifested in the revelation of the Spirit through the apostles; or as
Peter puts it, "them that preached the gospel to you by the Holy
Spirit sent forth from heaven" (1 Pet. 1:12).

Jesus claimed to be the truth as being "he in whom the truth is
summed up and impersonated" (GT on *aletheia*, 26). But John's readers had learned about Jesus by revelation of the Spirit through such
spokesmen for Christ as apostles and prophets (cf. 3:24b; 4:1). Their
knowledge had come "from the Spirit which he gave us" (3:24b; 4:13–
14). As the bearer, revealer and communicator of that truth, he is identified with the truth, and for that reason is presented as the primary
witness to Jesus Christ.

It was by means of this testimony of the Spirit that the meaning of
the cross was known and understood first by the original witnesses
(4:9–14) and then by others through them (1:1–4).

Three Witnesses (8)

My readers will acknowledge that I will usually keep working at
the connections of thought until I have something reasonable to offer. My "thinking through" series is all about tracing the course of
thought in various books of the Bible. But I must admit to being
stumped here. If all my work with the scriptures had been as puzzling as the chain of thought running through verses 5–12 I would
never have undertaken the task of trying to think through anything.
Even here I have tried to offer plausible solutions to difficulties. But
verse 8 is especially puzzling. What is it doing here? How does it
relate to what precedes? I do not know.

Verse 7 is not a problem. John is offering the testimony of the
Spirit as evidence of the assertions about Jesus in verses 5 and 6, namely,

proof that he is the Son of God, the one who came not only by the water of baptism but also by the blood of the cross. But after appealing to the Spirit as "the one who bears witness," suddenly we find John seeming to say: In fact, the witnesses are three, the Spirit, whose testimony was already mentioned (7), and the water and the blood, which were already mentioned (6), though not said to be witnesses.

Now *water* is a likely reference to Jesus' baptism by John the Baptist. In fact, the Spirit of God came upon Jesus in a visible form following the baptism of Jesus by John (Matt. 3:16), which was a prearranged sign by which John was to recognize the Christ (= Messiah) (John 1:31–33). Then the Father spoke out, acknowledging Jesus as his "beloved Son" (Matt. 3:17). Afterwards John would declare: "And I have seen, and have borne witness that this is the Son of God" (John 1:34). So Jesus' baptism in water is certainly strong testimony that Jesus is the Son of God.

But what about the *blood*, Jesus' sacrificial death on the cross? In what way does the death of Jesus offer testimony to the effect that Jesus is the Christ, the Son of God? It may have some reference to the account in John, in which "there came out blood and water" from the pierced side of Jesus. John is certainly emphatic about this event being witnessed by himself, on the basis of which he gave true testimony "so that you also may believe" (John 19:31–35). The testimony may be related to the denial of Jesus Christ "come in the flesh" (1 John 4:2). But another thought, which I do not think I have seen in the scholarly commentaries, is the point that is also emphatic in John to the effect that the crucifixion was the fulfillment of Old Testament expectation (John 19:28–37). Certainly it is true that the sufferings of the Christ were a subject of Old Testament prophecy (Luke 24:44–46; Acts 2:23; 3:18; 17:1–3; 26:22–23; 1 Pet. 1:10–11). So perhaps John is saying as over against opponents who denied that the Christ came "in the blood" as well as "in the water" (5:6): Not only did Jesus come by both water and blood, but in fact, he had to come in the blood in order to be the Christ of Old Testament expectation. His suffering and death, therefore, is a witness to his messiahship. The very thing that was for Jews a stumblingblock and for Greeks foolishness (1 Cor. 1:23) is presented as evidence that Jesus is the Christ, the Son of God.

This explanation seems plausible, although I must admit that John has not made this connection with the Old Testament in the context.

Another difficulty is that verse 8 begins with the word "For" (meaning because).[95] I see no connection at all with what immediately precedes (7). Westcott reaches all the way back to verse 5 for the connection. "This clause appears to give the reason for the main proposition in verse 5, that 'Jesus is the Son of God,' ... What has been said in v. 6 ... prepares the way for the assertion of this complete personal testimony, adequate according to the human standard: Deut. 19:15; comp. John 8:17ff." But this seems terribly awkward and forced to me. I have no explanation of the connection.

The last line of verse 8 is literally: "and the three are for[96] the one thing" (NASB margin). The point is that the three witnesses agree. The testimony of all three is to the same effect.[97]

Reasons for Accepting the Testimony of God (9–12)

"If we accept the testimony of men," John begins his final point, in which he sets forth powerful reasons for accepting the testimony of God. The testimony of God is not additional testimony added to the preceding testimony. The witnesses John has cited communicate the testimony of God. The point of verses 9–12 is not to add additional testimony, but to present reasons why the testimony already given ought to be accepted.

The "if" does not suggest doubt. We do indeed accept human testimony for the settlement of great issues. Our system of courts largely depends upon the acceptance of human testimony. Sometimes issues of life and death are decided on the ground of such testimony. But the conclusion drawn from this common practice is: "the testimony of God is greater"—i. e., more important or significant, more consequential, and therefore, with all the more reason to accept it. This explanation does not derive from the word *greater* itself, but from the context in which it is used.

---

[95] Grk *hoti*.

[96] Greek preposition *eis*, which could also be *to* or *towards*.

[97] "Are for the one thing, tend in the same direction, exist for the same object. They all work towards the same result, the establishing of the truth that Jesus is the Christ, the Son of God" (Brooke).

In such comparisons context determines the particular way in which one thing is greater than another. When John wrote: "God is greater than our heart" (3:20), the context indicates the meaning "greater in knowledge." The statement: "Greater is the one that is in you than the one that is in the world" (4:4) requires a similar meaning.

In this case the assertion is linked to what follows by the Greek conjunction *hoti*, meaning "because." John is going to justify his assertion by citing three reasons the testimony of God is greater:

1. The Subject of God's Testimony: "This is the testimony of God, that he has testified concerning his Son" (9b). When the subject on which God has given testimony is compared with the subjects on which human beings are required to testify, how can one doubt that the testimony of God is greater or more important?

2. The Implications of One's Response: "The one who believes on the Son of God has the testimony in himself" (10a). He has accepted the testimony, and it is therefore in his heart or mind. On the other hand, "the one who does not believe God [i. e., has not accepted his testimony] has made him a liar, because he has not believed in the testimony which God has testified concerning his Son" (10b). Can the implications of one's response to any other testimony be as great?

3. The Enormous Consequences of Unbelief: What this testimony amounts to is "that God gave us eternal life, and this life is in his Son [cf. 1:1–4]. The one who has the Son has the life; the one who does not have the Son of God does not have the life" (11–12). One's reaction to God's testimony is not a merely academic matter. It is a matter of life and death. Whether one will participate in eternal life depends on it. Can one's attitude toward any mere human testimony be as consequential?

John has fully established his point that the testimony of God is greater than any human testimony and demands acceptance by those who decide many questions on the basis of mere human testimony.

The closing portion of this epistle lays stress on Christian certainties. In an epistle from one of the original witnesses of Christ, in which the author has been at pains to explain where the lines are to be drawn, the difference between the truth and error, the true prophets and the false, the true children of God and the children of the devil, such a conclusion is certainly climactic. The closing section falls into two parts, in the first of which John explains that he has written to the readers in order that they may *know* that they have eternal life (13). After the development of this thought with some related material (14–17), a final passage (18–21) summarizing the great truth set forth in the epistle wraps it up by means of three assertions concerning the things *we know* for sure (18, 19, 20).

Purpose for Writing: Assurance of Eternal Life (13)

"These things I wrote[98] to you," John begins, "in order that[99] you may know that you have life, *the life that is* eternal,"[100] and concludes the sentence by identifying the persons who have eternal life, thus explaining why his readers are included among those who can be given such assurance: "you who believe on the name of the Son of God."

Does "these things" refer specifically to the immediately preceding material? Possibly. John had discussed the testimony that makes certain just who the person named Jesus really is (5–12), concluding that the testimony amounts to this, that God has given us eternal life in his Son, so that the person who has the Son, and only this person, has the life that is eternal (11–12). So this testimony is presented for the purpose of providing John's readers with assurance that they have eternal life. But in fact, this immediately preceding passage summarizes a great deal of the content of the whole epistle, including the prologue at

---

[98] Aorist tense in Greek.

[99] Greek *hina*.

[100] I have tried to preserve something of the Greek word order and emphasis. Following a common practice I have italicized added words.

the beginning (1:1–4), where the subject of apostolic testimony is said to be "the life, the eternal *life*, which was with the Father and was manifested to us" (2). One strong emphasis of the epistle has been upon how we know who does and does not have eternal life (3:13–15; cf. 2:25; 4:9). So it may be that verse 13 has the same function as the similar statement of purpose at the conclusion of John's Gospel (20:30–31). At the conclusion of both John explains the purpose of the book. The Gospel was written in order that people "may believe that Jesus is the Christ, the Son of God; and that believing (they) may have life in his name." The epistle was written to provide assurance to believers "on the name of the Son of God" that they have eternal life.

"That you may know!" John writes. Not feel, think, guess or imagine, but know. They could know it. They had certain knowledge, which rested on the ground of the testimony of the Spirit (5:7; cf. 3:24b; 4:12–13) communicated through the original witnesses of the Christ (1:1–4; 4:6, 14), or as otherwise put, the truth which the readers had heard from the beginning (2:20–24).

But why was such assurance necessary? Why would they doubt it? The answer is plain to see. False teachers had arisen, challenging the foundations of Christian faith. They were raising questions and doubts about exactly who this person named Jesus really was. Pay special attention to 2:25–26. Immediately following John's statement: "And this is the promise which he promised us, the life eternal" (25) he explains: "These things I have written to you concerning them that would lead you astray" (26). Indeed! They would deceive you concerning the very object and substance of your faith. But John has exposed these teachers as liars and antichrists and warned his readers that they must not listen to them, but keep to that which they had heard from the actual witnesses of Christ at the beginning (2:18–27). He had given them a certain test by which they could distinguish between the spirit of truth and the spirit of error (4:1–6). Thus they could know who Jesus really is, and knowing that, know also who has eternal life.

See at 2:23 for discussion of *the name of the Son of God*. As in the Old Testament (cf. Gen. 17:5; 29:31–45; 30:6–13, 18–24; 32:27–28; 35:10; 41:50–52), so in the New, the names of persons were significant because of their meaning (cf. John 1:42). The name of a person said who and what that person was. *The name of the Son of God* tells us who that person was, all that he has been shown to be. Thus here (and in 2:23) it is belief in the name of the Son of God, but in 5:5 it is simply belief "that Jesus is the Son of God."

Boldness in Prayer (14–15)

This certainty with regard to the possession of eternal life is accompanied by a boldness in the relationship with God: "And this is the boldness which we have toward him, that if we ask anything according to his will, he hears us: ..." (14). The Greek *parresia* occurs here for the fourth time, twice with regard to the judgment at the coming of Christ (2:28; 4:17) and twice with regard to prayer. Again (as in 2:21f) the original root idea of "freedom of speech" would seem to be prominent. Again, favorable response to prayer has conditions attached. In the previous passage John wrote: "and whatever we ask we receive of him, because we keep his commandments and do the things that are pleasing in his sight" (2:22). True believers are a people devoted to the will of God for their lives. When they come to God in prayer they seek his will and not just the fulfillment of selfish and worldly lusts (2:15–17). Like Jesus himself (Matt. 26:39, 42) they pray in submission to his will, wanting that before everything else. Even when their praying is uninformed and must be corrected by the Lord, they are happy to learn of their error and to submit themselves to the will of God which has their higher good in view (cf. 2 Cor. 12:7–10), as they have come to understand. Even in such cases they will feel that God has heard the deeper intent of their hearts.

He hears us refers to a favorable hearing as the continuation indicates: "... and if we know that he hears us whatever we ask, we know that we have the requests[101] which we have asked from him" (15). Some explain this to mean that although we do not already have in hand the thing we asked for, we know that it has already been approved by God. But when we consider the sort of requests illustrated in the following verse (16), the real explanation as to why such an assurance is given that we have the thing we asked lies in the nature of the thing asked. If we were asking for some material object we would not have to be told whether we had it. We would be able to see whether we had

---

[101] Grk *aitema*, the things asked for. The verb which occurs three times in verses 14 & 15 is *aiteo* (also in 3:22 & 5:16).

it. But John is thinking of such spiritual petitions as life or forgiveness for a sinning brother, and the only way we can be sure that we have obtained what we asked is for God to tell us.

Specific Application (16–17)

The climax of the passage (13–17) is reached with an example of the sort of thing one might ask, and this example would seem to indicate the main point to which the passage leads: "If anyone sees his brother sinning a sin which is not unto death, he shall (or will) ask, and he[103] shall give him life for them that sin not unto death" (16a). John does not say he ought to ask, but he shall (or will) ask. This asking is something that a disciple of Jesus will do. He does not want his brother to be lost. His love for his brother (cf. 3:16–17) moves him to ask for forgiveness (or life) on behalf of his brother.

This asking relates to a sin that is *not unto death*. The Greek preposition is *pros*, which would literally be *to* or *towards* death. The preposition "denotes direction towards a thing, or position and state looking towards a thing" and in this place is used "of the issue or end to which anything tends or leads" (GT, 541, 542) or "the result that follows a set of circumstances" (AG, 710).[104] The same preposition occurs in John 11:4 with regard to an illness that leads to (physical) death. Some scholars draw attention to Old Testament parallels which speak of sins that lead to death (Num. 18:22; Deut. 22:26; Is. 22:14). These are all references to physical death, and some think that may be what John has in mind here (cf. Acts 5:1–11; 1 Cor. 11:30). But throughout the epistle John's subject has been spiritual or eternal life (1:2; 2:25; 3:14–15; 4:9; 5:11–12), and the present passage began

---

[103] Literal translation. At first sight *he* would seem to refer to the same one doing the asking. The thought would then be that he gives life to the sinning brother by his prayers on his behalf. The parallel thought in James 5:19–20 proves that the idea is not all that far-fetched. Ultimately, of course, God alone has life in himself which can be imparted to others (John 5:21, 25–26; 1 Tim. 6:13, 16). For that reason many think *he* refers to God who is certainly the ultimate source of life (1 John 1:2; 2:25; 4:9; 5:11–12), although this view results in some awkward grammar.

[104] "*Pros thanaton* must, of course, denote a tendency in the direction of death, and not an attained result" (Brooke).

with an assurance that the readers were in possession of eternal life (5:13). The life to be given in answer to a brother's prayer (5:16) would seem to be defined as spiritual life in accord with these uses. John has said (in 3:14) that love of the brothers is evidence "that we have passed out of death into life." "He who does not love remains in death." The next verse speaks of "eternal life." So the likelihood is that *a sin to death* is a reversal of the process described in 3:14. It is a sin by which one passes out of life into death.

Before venturing an explanation, we must get the remainder of John's explanation before us. He continues by saying there is such a thing as sin unto death, and further still, that he is not saying that one should pray for a brother who is guilty of that type sin (16b). Some point out that John does not forbid prayer even in this case. But is that not the implication of a passage on prayer that began with a reference to asking according to the will of God (14), and then continues with this illustration? John would seem to indicate that it is useless to pray for one guilty of this type sin.

To be sure, John continues (in 17): "All unrighteousness[104] is sin: and there is sin that does not lead to death."

The explanation of sin that leads to death should start with what this epistle has taught us about the forgiveness of sin. "If we walk in the light," John began, "the blood of Jesus his Son cleanses us from all sin" (1:7). Sin unto death is plainly that of one who does not walk in the light. "If we confess our sins, he is faithful and righteous to forgive us our sins, and to cleanse us from all unrighteousness" (1:9). Sin unto death is that of one who will not confess his sins, but instead, claims to have no sin (1:8) or "that we have not sinned" (1:10).

John wrote in order that his readers may not sin (2:1a). But if anyone does, provision has been made through Jesus Christ for forgiveness (2:1–2). Jesus Christ manifested his love by laying down his life for us (3:16). God manifested his love by sending "his only begotten Son into the world that we might live through him" (4:9). God "loved us, and sent his Son as the propitiation for our sins" (4:10). The one who has the Son of God has eternal life in him (5:11–12). So John has taught that

---

[104] Grk *adikia* is any wrongdoing; any act that is contrary to what is right; or, one might say, that is in conflict with the character of God (2:29; 3:7).

though Christians may fall into sin, forgiveness is possible for those who walk in the light of the revelation of God in Christ. And those who are in this fellowship will have a concern for each other, leading them to approach God about a brother whom they see sinning a sin. John says life will be given to this sinning brother, provided his sin is not unto death. Of course he himself will also need to confess his sin and seek forgiveness, once the light of the truth has revealed his sin to him.

But John has written about some who abandoned the light. They had evidently been associated with the apostles, but did not really belong, and made it manifest by departing from the apostolic fellowship (2:18–19). These people were antichrists who denied that Jesus is the Christ, and who therefore had neither the Father nor the Son (2:22–23). They did not confess Jesus come in the flesh, and they were not of God (4:2–3). They denied that it was the Son of God who died on the cross (4:9–10). They had abandoned the light and had committed sin that leads to death. There was no use praying for such as these, for they had rejected the only way of salvation. One might pray that they have a change of heart. But he could not ask God to give them life as long as they continued in their darkness.

So this passage, coming so near the end of the epistle, seems to be climactic indeed, and is explained in the light of the entire content of the epistle.

Final Summary of the Great Truth Set Forth in This Epistle: Three Things We Know

This epistle has provided certainty concerning the truth of the gospel as over against the teaching of false prophets whose errors would tend to disturb the hearts of the true people of God. John has set forth the truth as it comes from the original witnesses to the Christ. He makes clear the difference between the truth and error. He indicates where the lines are drawn between the children of God and the children of the devil. The epistle concludes with three great assertions of the certainty we have in Christ Jesus, summarizing the main points of the epistle. Three times John declares: "We know!" Thus the epistle closes with a climactic note of certainty such as has run as a thread throughout its content.

The Security of One Begotten of God (18)

"We know," says John, "that everyone who is begotten from God does not sin, ..." We have had this thought before in First John 3:6, 9. The second of these verses assigns the reason: "because his seed remains in him." God has planted his seed in him through his word (cf. 1 Pet. 1:23). He is a partaker of the nature of the God who is righteous (2:29), entirely pure (3:3) and sinless (3:5).

The statement comes as a surprise on the heels of John's discussion of how a brother, defined as one begotten of God (5:1 with 4:21), a child of God (5:2), might be observed "sinning a sin" (5:16). John certainly cannot mean that a child of God does not commit any sins. We have seen evidence to the contrary not only in this immediate passage, but also in 1:6–2:2 and in 3:3. So the point, I think, is that when a child of God sins he acts contrary to his nature; sinful behavior is a contradiction of his nature. As in 3:6 & 9, the statement is an assertion that sin must not be taken lightly. It goes against all that a person is as a child of God.[105]

---

[105] The verb (actually participle) is in the perfect tense, which describes an action which took place in the past, but continues to have its effect in the

footnote continued on next page

The ground of his security is stated in the second half of the verse: "but the one who was begotten[106] from God keeps him, and the evil one does not touch him." Some of the best scholars understand the one begotten from God to be Jesus, and that is probably the correct explanation.[107] The only place in the writings of John where the Greek for begotten[108] is applied to Jesus is at John 18:37, a reference to the birth by which he entered into the world. But it is also applied to either the conception or birth of Jesus in Matthew 1:16, 20; 2:1, 4; & Luke 1:35. So I see no reason why the term could not be applied to Jesus.

Furthermore, Jesus is said to keep his disciples in John 17:12 and again in Revelation 3:10. It will be worthwhile to consider the usage in John 17:12 because it proves that the keeping is not unconditional. Jesus was speaking of the twelve apostles: "While I was with them, I was keeping them in your name which you have given me; and I guarded them, and not one of them perished, but the son of perdition, that the Scripture might be fulfilled." The keeping and guarding was not unconditional. One of those who were kept and guarded perished. The keeping was conditional, dependent not only on the power of the Keeper, but also on the faith of those kept (cf. 1 Pet. 1:5).

As we have so often done before, we can reach back to earlier passages for the understanding of this one. John has not only set forth the condition of being kept by the Lord Jesus, but he has also explained the keeping—what the Lord is doing to preserve those who are his

---

present: Everyone who has been begotten in the past and now stands as begotten of God. So the idea is that everyone who has been begotten from God in the past and now stands begotten of God does not sin. If he does sin, his present behavior would contradict the experience of the past. It would not remain effective in the present.

[106] Not perfect tense as before, but aorist (action taking place at a point in the past).

[107] See Marshall, 352, n. 37 for a summary of the arguments. Weighty manuscript evidence exists for the reading *heauton* (himself) instead of *auton* (him). But it seems more likely that an original *him* would be changed to the easier reading *himself* rather than the other way around. My explanation is supported in the following translations: ASV margin, RSV, NASB, NIV; also in scholarly commentaries such as Westcott, Brooke, Dodd and Bruce.

[108] Grk *gennao*.

from the evil one. "If we walk in the light, as he is in the light, we have fellowship one with another, and the blood of Jesus his Son cleanses us from all sin" (1:7). True, we must deal with our sins in the right way when they are exposed by the light (1:8–10). But given that we do so, provision has been made in case children of God fall into sin (2:1–2). The Lord Jesus wants his disciples to refrain from sin, and thus his apostle writes to them in order that they may not sin (2:1a). But in the event they do fall into sin he pleads their case with the Father on the ground of his own propitiatory sacrifice (2:1b–2a), and thus the evil one cannot touch them.

So if we have read through this epistle with good attention, we not only understand the security of the children of God, but we will also avoid presumptuous and false conclusions from it.

The Difference Between Children of God and the World (19)

We know something else. "We know that we are from[109] God, and the whole world lies in the evil one." GT, 343 explains the use of the verb *keimai* in this verse: "lies in the power of the evil one, i. e. is held in subjection by the devil."[110] See Luke 4:6 for the idea. Reference to the sphere of his rule and control. Westcott explains: "is placed in the sphere of his influence."

"Christians are conscious, immediately and intuitively, of the difference between the power which dominates their life and that which controls absolutely the life, intellectual and moral, of the world, i. e. of the world of men so far as they remain estranged from God" (Brooke).

This verse too summarizes material that has been fully discussed in an earlier passage (2:28–ch. 3). If we recall what was already put before us in this earlier passage, we will understand the implications of what is so briefly summarized in this verse. This difference between the children of God and the world has implications not only with regard to the behavior that must characterize children of God, but it also explains the attitude of the world toward them. Recall the fuller discussion in the earlier passage.

---

[109] Grk *ek*, out of. The source of our existence is God.

[110] AG, 426 is similar: "the world lies in (the power of) the evil one," but suggesting another possibility, the idea of being dependent on one.

The True God (20)

The last assertion is set in contrast with what precedes by the adversative conjunction *de*: "We know that we are from God, and the whole world lies in the evil one." We know that. But we also know something else. We know who the true God is. Here's how:

"But we know that the Son of God has come, and has given us understanding (or insight) in order to[112] know the one who is true; and we are in him that is true, in his Son Jesus Christ." The Greek *dianoia* refers to the mind as the faculty of understanding, and then understanding (or insight) itself. The coming of the Son of God brought understanding enabling us to know the one that is true. God is true (Grk *alethes*) as always speaking the truth (John 3:33; Rom. 3:4). But he is also true (Grk *alethinos* here) in another sense, namely, as being genuine and real; entirely fulfilling the idea indicated by the name, in contrast to false gods which have no real existence at all.

Furthermore, John continues, "we are in him that is true, in his Son Jesus Christ." That is to say that we are in union or fellowship (cf. 1:1–4) with the true God, and the way in which that fellowship is realized is *in his Son Jesus Christ*. The phrase describes "the method in which union with God is realized. ... The words supply a needed explanation. It is in virtue of their relation to Christ, and their fellowship with Him, that Christians realize their fellowship with God" (Brooke). "So far as Christians are united with Christ, they are united with God" (Westcott). Thus the point approximates the one made earlier: "he that confesses the Son has the Father also" (2:23).

"This one," John concludes, referring to the God revealed in Jesus Christ, "is the true God, and eternal life" (20b).

Final Warning (21)

"Little children," John concludes, "guard yourselves from idols." I doubt that John means "to guard one's self from all manner of fellowship with heathen worship" (GT, 174 on *eidolon*). John has not dealt with idolatry in the literal sense, but refers here to any false concept of God. He has dealt with teachers who claimed to have God without the Son and branded them the liar and the antichrist (2:22–23). The true

---

[112] Grk *hina*.

God has been revealed in Christ Jesus, and any other concept of God is not the true God, but an idol.[112]

We know! John concludes. From first to last he has dealt with the certainty about God that has been manifested in Christ Jesus. Unbelieving philosophers may be like a blind man searching in a totally dark room for a black cat that is not even there. *But we know!* The "bishop" whose book I referred to at the beginning may not know whether his god is superior to the god of the other fellow. But we do. We know!

---

[112] "All the false images of God which men have made for themselves instead of accepting the true revelation of Him given in His Son. The expression embraces all false conceptions of God" (Brooke).

The Second Epistle of John

It is not certain that the second epistle was actually the second to be written. It has the appearance of providing advance warning with regard to the false teaching dealt with in First John, much as Second Peter provides advance warning with regard to the teachers dealt with in Jude.[113] As in First John, stress is laid upon two subjects, the truth of the gospel and brotherly love.

Salutation (1–3)

The author identifies himself as "the elder" (1), as also in Third John (1). He provides no other self-identification and evidently the readers were expected to know him by this term. The Greek *presbuteros* means an older man and sometimes is used literally. But in ancient days leaders were usually older men. The Jewish Sanhedrin had its elders, and Paul appointed "elders in every church" (Acts 14:23). But a plurality of such elders were appointed in each local body, and it is unlikely that one of them would refer to himself as *the* elder. The term is used for "elders" in ancient times, as in Hebrews 11:2; and we read about "the tradition of the elders" in Matthew 15:2 & Mark 7:3, 5. A number of scholars have referred to Papias' use of the term elders for the apostles, and the author of First John has certainly identified himself with the original witnesses of Christ (1:1–4).[114] Bornkamm cites Papias, Irenaeus and others who use the term elders "for members of the older generation who are regarded as mediators of the authentic tradition and reliable teachers" (TDNT, VI, 676). It seems odd, as Marshall points out, that one of this group would refer to himself as "the elder." It seems more like a term others would use for him, than one he would use for himself. But if it had become a kind of standard designation among the readers for the author, it may not be so unnatural that he would adopt their term for himself. The singular would be natural if the author were the last survivor of such a group or the one

---

[113] See J. A. T. Robinson, *Redating the New Testament*, 285f.
[114] See the quotation in Marshall, 42f.

"elder" who had been associated with the readers and was so called by them. Perhaps the usage in these epistles can be compared to the way the author of an article in a church bulletin might be simply identified as "The Pastor," no further identification being necessary.[115]

The letter is addressed "to the elect lady and her children" (1). The Greek terms for *elect lady* have sometimes been understood as the proper name of an individual, either *the Lady Electa* or *the elect Kuria*. But this view has been discussed at length in the scholarly commentaries and found unlikely. *Elect* means chosen, and *kuria* is the word for lady which corresponds to the Greek word for lord, *kurios*. It is much more likely that *the elect lady* is intended as a collective term referring to a local congregation. *Her children* would be the individual members. Consider the way the singular and the plural are interchanged in verses 4, 5, 8, 10, 12 & 13. The lady is addressed (in 5), but then a plural "you" is used with reference to her (in 6b, 8 & 12). Another argument that seems conclusive is based on verse 13, where greetings are communicated from "the children of your elect sister." As in both Old Testament (Is. 54:1–7, 13) and New (Gal. 4:26), a city with its inhabitants is portrayed by the imagery of a mother with her children, so here the same imagery is used for churches and their members.[116] See First Peter 5:13 for a close parallel to the present usage.

This lady with her children are then described: *whom I love in truth*. Though some have taken *in truth* to mean truly, or with a love that is genuine, the repeated reference to truth in what follows surely demands that *truth* be defined with reference to the truth of the gospel (cf. 1 John 2:21; 3:19). Truth, reality defined by divine revelation, is the sphere in which this love is exercised.

Furthermore, the author is not alone. This love for the chosen lady and her children is shared by *all who know the truth*. This love, the

---

[115] "Just how we are to understand the words *ho presbuteros*, applied to himself by the author of the two smallest Johannine letters 2 J 1; 3 J 1, remains in doubt. But in any case it is meant to indicate a position of great dignity *the elder*" (AG, 700).

[116] Compare verses that portray the church as the bride of Christ (2 Cor. 11:2; Eph. 5:22–33).

author continues, is *on account of the truth* (2). It is the truth of the gospel that has brought about this bond of love in truth. The truth of divine revelation has cemented together all who know the truth in the bond of love. They love each other on account of the revealed truth which they share.

The truth is then further described. It is the truth "which remains in us, and shall be with us for ever" (2). The truth is the word of God, the word of good news, *which lives and remains* (1 Pet. 1:22–25).

Observe that the truth is described in the same terms Jesus had used to describe the Holy Spirit (John 14:16–17). Then notice that the Spirit has been identified with the truth (in 1 John 5:7) just as Jesus himself had claimed to be the truth (John 14:6). Jesus would not remain on earth for ever, but would ascend to the Father (John 14:12). But he would not leave the apostles entirely alone like orphan children, but would send the Holy Spirit as "another helper" (John 14:16–18). The Spirit of truth would reveal the whole truth to the apostles (John 16:12–15), and would then remain in the apostles, and in fact all who know the truth, and would be with them for ever through the medium of the divine revelation communicated to them (2 John 2). The Spirit would not remain personally and directly with the Christians any more than Jesus himself did, but would be with them through the medium of the divine revelation left by him.

Now the salutation (3). The combination grace, mercy, and peace occurs in Paul's epistles to Timothy (1 Tim. 1:2; 2 Tim. 1:2). But whereas they appear as a wish in these epistles, here the greeting takes the form of an assurance: "Grace, mercy, peace[117] shall be with us," with the source added: "from God the Father, and from Jesus Christ, the Son of the Father," and finally, definition of the sphere in which these blessings are realized: "in truth and love." Grace, mercy and peace are assured to us, from God the Father and from Jesus Christ the Son in the sphere of the truth and love. We must remain within this

---

[117] Grace is favor or lovingkindness manifested toward the guilty and undeserving; mercy, "kindness or good will towards the miserable and afflicted, joined with a desire to relieve them" (GT on *eleos*, 203); peace, the condition of harmony that results.

sphere in order to have the blessings. Truth and love are the subjects that will be elaborated in the main body of the letter.

Counsel and Warning (4–11)

First the expression of joy (4). The author tells the elect lady: "I felt great joy to find of your children [literally, meaning some of them] walking in truth, even as we received commandment from the Father." I doubt that he means to imply that some of them were not so walking, as some think. Nothing is said about any of her children except these. In Third John 3 he mentions brothers who had come to him, and that may suggest how he found some of the elect lady's children walking in truth. Perhaps they had paid him (or the church where he was) a visit. Or perhaps he had run across them in the city. In any case, it caused him great joy to learn that they were walking in truth according to the commandment received from the Father. The next two verses indicate that he is referring to the command to love one another. This commandment was communicated through Jesus Christ (cf. John 13:34–35; 15:12), but ultimately came from the Father.

This discovery about some of the elect lady's children (meaning members of the church being addressed) had happened in the past. And *now* he had a request to make of the church (5). But it was not as though he was sending a new commandment (cf. 1 John 2:7–11). It was the same old commandment they had from the beginning. It had been communicated through Christ himself. It was the old commandment "that we love one another."

I doubt that this request implies anything about the state of the church. In the case of Paul, at least, it was a request that could have been made even if he knew that they were already obeying this commandment (cf. 1 Thess. 4:9–10). But churches can always be exhorted to do better; and as we shall soon see (7) John has special reason for sending this request at the time.

John goes on to define love: "And this is love, that we should walk according to his commandments. This is the commandment, even as you (pl.) heard from the beginning, that you (pl.) should walk in it" (6). The plural proves that the lady being addressed is a collective. John is addressing a church.

110

He is speaking of love for one another (5). So it may seem strange to have him explain this love as a matter of walking after God's commandments. Would not this explanation better suit love for God? Well, in fact, the keeping of the commandments is the way love for God is shown. But we must remember what John has written about how one knows that he loves the children of God. We know it "when we love God and do his commandments" (1 John 5:2f). The fact is, these commandments deal largely with how we treat each other. The test of our love is not how we feel or what we claim. We know that we love the children of God when we obey the commandments God has given about how to treat them. So Second John 6 ties right in with what John teaches in First John 5:2f.

The plural "commandments" refers to the various expressions of love for the brothers. The singular "commandment" refers to the command to love one another, which embodies all the "commandments." Compare Paul's exposition of this subject in Romans 13:8–10.

Now the reason for an exhortation to give attention to this old commandment (7). Verse 7 begins with the conjunction *hoti*, which means because. It assigns a reason for walking in the commandment to love one another: "For many deceivers went out[118] into the world, ..." They went out, as on a mission. Who are these deceivers? "... they that do not confess Jesus Christ coming in the flesh. This is the deceiver and the antichrist." Compare First John 2:18–22 & 4:2–3.

The confession is similar to First John 4:2, but the tense is different. There the perfect tense is used: Jesus Christ having come in the flesh. Here Jesus Christ coming in the flesh renders a present participle. By the use of the present tense "the confession is taken out of all connection with time and made timeless. In the First Epistle stress was laid on the historical fact and its permanent consequences. Here the writer regards it as a continuous fact. The Incarnation is not only an event in history. It is an abiding truth. It is the writer's view that humanity has been taken up into the Deity. The union is permanent and abiding" (Brooke). Westcott is similar.

Again we see (as in 1 John 2:18–22) that the singular is intended collectively, including a whole class of individuals. The "many de-

---

[118] Aorist tense.

ceivers" are said to be "the deceiver and the antichrist." So according to John the antichrist was not a single individual, but any teacher who denies the truth about Jesus.

But what is the connection with the exhortation to love one another (4–6)? John is assigning a reason for heeding the command to love one another, and that reason is the deceivers who do not confess Jesus Christ coming in the flesh. Perhaps the thought is that such teachers threaten the unity between brothers. They are "likely to prove destructive to the exercise of mutual love among Christians."

Another possibility is that their denial of the reality of the incarnation undermines the foundation of Christian love. It was the manifestation of God's love at the cross that moves Christians to love each other. "We love because he first loved us" (1 John 4:7–21). But if it was not the Son of God that died on the cross as the propitiation for our sins (1 John 4:9–11), then the cross ceases to be such a great manifestation of love, and the reason we love each other ceases to exist. The error taught by these deceivers is not merely academic. It destroys the foundation of the Christian life.[119]

Now comes the warning (8–11). "Watch yourselves," John writes, "that you not lose (or destroy)[120] the things we have accomplished, but that you receive a full reward" (8). Some manuscripts have *the things you have accomplished*, which is probably not the correct reading, but an attempt on the part of a copyist to bring the pronouns into agreement. *The things we have accomplished* most likely refers to the apostolic work. The Greek *ergazomai* means to work out, achieve or accomplish. Consult First Cor. 3:10–15 for the idea of a teacher losing his work, and Romans 14:20 for the work of God in a person being overthrown or destroyed (cf. v. 15b).[121]

The continuation in verses 9–11 explains just how much is at stake when these teachers appear, and how important it is to hold to the true teaching of Christ. "Whoever goes onward and does not remain in the

---

[119] These two points are found in Brooke.

[120] The Greek verb is *apollumi*, on which see GT, 64 & AG, 95.

[121] For *reward*, see *misthos* in GT, 415 & AG, 523. Cf. Ruth 2:12 for *a full reward*.

teaching of the Christ does not have God: ..." (9a). The verb *proago* is
literally to lead (*ago*) before (*pro*). It is used in Mark 11:9 of those who
"went before" as opposed to those who followed. It is used of Jesus
"going before" or "preceding" his followers (Mark 10:32; 14:28; 16:7).
John describes people who are not followers. They take the lead; they
go out ahead. He speaks of "progressives," teachers with "advanced"
views. In fact they go "too far" (AG, 702); they go beyond the teaching of the Christ. They do not "remain in the teaching of the Christ."[122]

But is *the teaching of the Christ* teaching about the Christ (objective genitive), as some think, making reference to verse 7? Or is it
teaching that comes from Christ (subjective genitive)? Grammar does
not decide this question. Either meaning is grammatically possible.
The question must be decided on the basis of (a) context and (b) usage. With regard to usage, the relevant passages are those which use
the word teaching or doctrine in connection with persons. The evidence of usage would seem to be consistent. To begin with the writings of John, *my teaching* (in John 7:16) is the teaching Jesus was
doing (vv. 14–17); so also John 18:19 (cf. context of vv. 20 & 21).
The teaching of Balaam is what he taught (Rev. 2:14). So also *the
teaching of the Nicolaitans* (Rev. 2:15).

It is no different in other writings. *His teaching* (in Matt. 7:28) is the
teaching Jesus was doing. So also in Mark 4:2 & Luke 4:32. Finally, *the
apostles' teaching* (in Acts 2:42) is that which they were doing.

So New Testament usage would seem to favor the view that the
teaching of Christ is the teaching which derives from him. But what
about context? Does anything in context require a meaning different
from the normal usage of the New Testament? I think not. Begin with
the takeoff point (v. 6) with which the whole warning (7–11) is connected, and compare the idea of walking in the commandment (6) with

---

[122] The KJV (whosoever transgresseth) actually translates the variant reading, a
participle formed from the verb *parabaino*. Brooke seems to have the facts:
"The sarcastic reference of *proagon* to the claims of false teachers to the
possession of a higher knowledge and more progressive intelligence was naturally
misunderstood. The *parabainon* of the *Receptus* was the inevitable result. What
was not understood had to be corrected into an intelligible commonplace. If this
were the true text, we should have to supply as object *ten didachen* from the
following *en te didache*. But the originality of *proagon* is obvious."

the idea of remaining in the teaching of Christ (9). Add also the call for obedience to the commandment "which we had from the beginning" (5f), which recalls the emphasis of First John on sticking with the thing heard from the beginning (1:1–4; 2:7, 24, 27; 3:11; 4:6).

Whoever does not remain in the teaching of Christ, John writes, does not have God. Compare the introduction and the conclusion to First John. The apostolic testimony is the means by which one enters into fellowship with the apostles, which is a fellowship with the Father and the Son (1 John 1:1–4). We know the true God through the understanding communicated by the Son of God, so that one who rejects the teaching of Christ does not have God, but an idol, a false concept of God (5:20–21). Consult also 2:23, which is followed by an exhortation to let remain in you "that which you heard from the beginning," which is the means by which they "remain in the Son and in the Father" (v. 24).

John adds: "The one who remains in the teaching, that one has both the Father and the Son" (9b). Compare First John 2:23–24. One cannot have the Father without the Son. But the one who remains in the teaching by which God is made known (cf. 1 John 5:20) has both the Father and the Son.

The facts being such as indicated in verse 9, John gives the following counsel: "If anyone comes to you and does not bring this teaching, do not receive him into the house and do not give him greeting" (10). Plainly John is referring to teachers who come with a teaching which they want to communicate to the church (Brooke). In Third John the writer speaks of welcoming teachers of the truth, showing hospitality to them and supplying their needs for the journey (5–8). But no such welcome is to be extended to one who does not bring the true teaching of Christ. The Greek for giving him greeting is more literally: to say to him "rejoice" or "be glad."[123] Do not wish him joy.

The reason follows: "for the one who wishes him joy shares his evil works" (11). The Greek verb *koinoneo* means to have fellowship (*koinonia*) with or to become a partner. The one who wishes the false

___

[123] Grk verb *chairo*, GT, 663f & AG, 873f. For such greetings compare Acts 15:23; 23:26; Jas. 1:1; each verse referring to the greeting at the beginning of a letter.

teacher well or in any way provides support for him becomes a partner and an ally with him in the promotion of evil.

The harsh use that has often been made of verses 9–11 prompt me to express the view that these verses do not refer to everyone who misunderstands some teaching of Christ, while showing respect generally for the teaching of Christ. The teachers John has in view have abandoned the teaching of Christ. They have gone beyond this teaching by which God is revealed. They therefore do not have God.

Conclusion (12–13)

There was much more to say, but the author did not want to put it in a letter.[124] He hoped to visit "the elect lady and her children" and to speak face to face, literally *mouth to mouth*,[125] as in the Greek Old Testament at Numbers 12:8. His purpose is "that our joy may be made full." Meantime, greetings are communicated from "the children of your elect sister," referring to the people making up the congregation where John was.

---

[124] Grk *chartes* refers to the paper made from the papyrus plant (AG, 879). Grk *melan* is "the neuter of the adjective *melas*," meaning black (VED).

[125] Grk *stoma*. First Cor. 13:12 does have the expression "face to face."

The Third Epistle of John

Like the second epistle, the third is from an author identified as "the Elder." (See note on Second John 1.) Third John is addressed "to Gaius the beloved." The name is born by a number of men in the New Testament: (a) A man from Macedonia (Acts 19:29); (b) another from Derbe (Acts 20:4);[126] (c) a man from Corinth, baptized by Paul (1 Cor. 1:14), later Paul's host when he wrote the epistle to the Romans (Rom. 16:23). No evidence connects the Gaius to whom Third John was addressed with either of these men. We know no more about him than is found in this epistle.

The description is the same which had been applied to the elect lady and her children in Second John: "whom I love in truth." Again, John's usage of the word truth in these epistles points to the truth revealed in Christ Jesus as the sphere in which this love was exercised, rather than simply meaning truly. Again, compare the note on Second John 1.

The Report of Gaius' Faithfulness (2–4)

Like many ancient letters, this one begins with a wish[127] that Gaius may prosper or be successful[128] and be in health[129] in accordance with the way his soul prospers, referring to his spiritual state (2). Would that it could be so with all of us! Gaius' spiritual prosperity is illustrated in the following verses.

John elaborates (in 3) by speaking of the great joy he felt at the coming of brothers who testify "to your truth, even as you walk in truth." "The present tense of the participles may imply that more than one occasion is meant. The Presbyter, then, would be a person who

---

[126] Both of these were associated with Paul as traveling companions.

[127] The verb *euchomai* may mean either to pray or to wish, but in the case of the former we would expect *to God* to be attached. See GT, 264; AG, 329.

[128] Grk *euodoo*, GT, 260 & AG, 323.

[129] Besides this verse, Grk *hugiaino* is used literally of physical health in Luke 5:31; 7:10; 15:27. In the pastoral epistles it is used of soundness of doctrine and life. See GT, 634 & AG, 832.

was accustomed to receive traveling Christians, and their reports about the journey. Gaius would have been showing hospitality over a period of time and not only in this emergency when Diotrephes has refused to show hospitality" (Brown).[130]

Your truth is perhaps to be explained in light of Second John 2 as *the truth which is in him* as manifested by his walk in the truth, which is in turn explained by his hospitable treatment toward traveling preachers who came by on missions for the truth (3–8).

"I have no greater joy," John continues, "than this,[131] that I hear about my children walking in the truth" (4). *My children* may indicate John's converts (cf. 1 Cor. 4:14–17; 1 Tim. 1:2; 2 Tim. 1:2; Titus 1:4). But others think it may only indicate spiritual dependents.

Gaius' Faithful Work (5–8)

Gaius is commended for doing "a faithful thing whatever you work toward the brothers and (even) strangers" (5)—explained in verses 7–8 as traveling preachers in need of support. These brothers had testified to the love shown them by Gaius "before the church" (6a). John knew about the work of these brothers and probably had sent them on their mission, just as Paul sent out various coworkers as an extension of his apostolic work (cf. Phil. 2:19–24; 1 Thess. 3:1–10; 1 Tim. 1:3; 2 Tim. 4:1; Titus 1:5; 3:12). See what follows.

Gaius had done a faithful work toward such spokesmen for the truth in the past, and John encourages him to continue (6b). Apparently he had sent these men again, for he writes: "whom you will do well to send forth on their journey worthily of God." The Greek *propempo* means "to send forward, bring on the way, accompany or escort" (GT, 541). For this sense see Acts 20:38 & 21:5. But it also means: *"help on one's journey* with food, money, by arranging for companions, means of travel, etc.; *send on one's way"* (AG, 709). The present passage (cf. v. 7) is one

---

[130] Similarly Westcott, Marshall and others, including Brooke: "The tense almost precludes the reference of the words to a single occasion, ... They suggest rather the means by which the Elder kept himself in touch with the Churches for whose welfare he regarded himself as responsible, and over which he exercised his supervision."

[131] Literally, *these things*, perhaps referring to plural reports.

of two that illustrates this application. The other is Titus 3:13, which reads in part: "Set forward ... on their journey diligently, that nothing be wanting to them." The other occurrences of the verb are Acts 15:3; Rom. 15:24; 1 Cor. 16:6, 11; & 2 Cor. 1:16.

Worthily of God means *in a manner appropriate to men on a mission for God.* As Marshall writes: Those on a mission for God were not to be treated like beggars, "and so bring discredit on the name of the God to whom they were looking for their support."

"For" (Grk *gar*) introduces the reason these men were to be so treated: "on behalf of the Name they went forth, taking nothing from the Gentiles" (7). They did not ask for support from the Gentiles that they were trying to win for Christ. "Freely you received, freely give," said Jesus, as he sent the twelve out on their mission (Matt. 10:8). But such men were to be supported by established Christians who understood the nature of their mission.

The Name, used absolutely as in Acts 5:42, probably refers to the name of Jesus Christ. Brown is inclined to combine God and Christ, on account of the oneness that exists between the two. The one true God has been revealed in the Son (cf. 1 John 5:20).

A conclusion follows, introduced by the Greek *oun*: "We [emphatic in Greek, in contrast with the Gentiles] therefore ought to welcome (or to receive hospitably)[132] such men, that we may become fellow-workers for the truth" (8). By providing material support for such men we join with them in spreading the truth revealed in Christ Jesus.

The Evil Works of Diotrephes (9–12)

Over against the faithful work done by Gaius for the truth stands the evil of a man named Diotrephes. "I wrote something to the church," John begins (9a). Possibly the Elder refers to Second John. That is the view of G. G. Findlay[133] and J. A. T. Robinson considers it

---

[132] Grk *hupolambano*: "to receive hospitably, welcome" (GT, 643); "receive as a guest, support" (AG, 845). "The basic sense is 'to take from below,' 'to catch up.' Hence (in this verse) 'to take up someone (protectively).' This does not mean only hospitable reception, but carries the thought of protecting those who are persecuted" (Delling in TDNT, IV, 15). Brown agrees.

[133] *Fellowship in the Life Eternal*, 5f.

"not at all impossible."[134] Others think it is more likely an epistle which has not survived, perhaps destroyed by Diotrephes, in which John was urging the church to welcome teachers of the truth, along the lines of his words to Gaius (5–8).

Diotrephes is described as a man who loves to be first, to hold first place[135] among the brothers making up the church (9b). Being a man of selfish ambition, John continues, "he does not receive us." The same verb is used again in verse 10: he does not "receive the brothers," referring to the hospitable reception of such messengers of truth sent out by John as described in verses 5–8. But in verse 9 the non-reception accounts for the attitude Diotrephes took, or was expected to take, toward the letter sent to the church. "He does not receive us" and therefore would pay no attention to a letter from John. The letter was addressed to the church, but Diotrephes seems to have been in position to impose his will upon the church. The letter to the church may have been delivered to him, and perhaps he did not even let the church know about it.

The plural *us* would seem to refer to John with his colleagues, the apostolic witnesses (cf. 1 John 1:1–4). Diotrephes was so jealous of his own position and prerogatives that he set himself up against the authority of the apostles. Some find it hard to imagine that anyone in the church would challenge the authority of an apostle. But we must remember that Paul had challenges raised with regard to his apostleship, as indicated especially in Second Corinthians and Galatians.

Some point out that Diotrephes is not directly said to sympathize with the false teaching warned against in Second John. The problem, they say, arose from personal ambition and protection of this man's position and prerogatives. But I am not so sure. See below.

"On account of this,"[136] John continues, "if I come, I will bring to remembrance[137] his works which he does" (10)—as GT says, "with implied censure." John intended to expose this man's evil works before the church and to hold him accountable for them, bringing to bear

---

[134] *Redating the New Testament*, 288. It is also the view of Theodore Zahn in his *Introduction to the New Testament*, III, 378.

[135] Grk *philoproteuo*, GT, 654 & AG, 860.

[136] Grk *dia touto*.

[137] Grk *hupomimnesko*, GT, 644 & AG, 846.

the full weight of his authority (cf. 2 Cor. 10:10:1–11; 13:1). Three of these works are described in the remainder of verse 10:

No. 1: The first charge is that this man was talking idle nonsense against us, or making unjustified accusations against us.[138]

No. 2: Not satisfied[139] with these idle words, he adds deeds to words: he does not receive the brothers, the messengers of truth sent by John.

No. 3: He forbids, hinders or prevents[140] those who would receive such brothers and throws them out[141] of the church. What a tyrant!

This is serious business. This man had risen up against the authority of an apostle. He had refused faithful teachers sent out to teach truth and oppose the deceivers. He had brought pressures to bear to keep any other Christian from extending support to these teachers.

These teachers sent by John needed and deserved the support of faithful brothers. With Diotrephes preventing the church from filling the need, John writes this epistle to Gaius, calling upon him to fill it as he had in the past. Was John putting Gaius at risk of the wrath of Diotrephes? We cannot be sure. Perhaps Gaius was not in the same church as Diotrephes, but in a nearby house church or small congregation. In any case, the interests of truth required that he not be intimidated by the likes of Diotrephes.

After the description of the character and works of Diotrephes, John gives counsel to Gaius: "Beloved, do not imitate the evil, but the good. He that does good is from God;[142] he that does evil has not seen God" (11). In a sense, of course, no one has seen God (John 1:18; 5:37; 6:46; 1 John 4:12). John is probably speaking of the revelation of God in Christ (cf. John 14:9). The doer of evil does not know God as he is revealed in Christ.

---

[138] See GT, 655 & AG, 862 on the Greek verb *phluareo*.

[139] Grk *arkeo*, GT, 73 & AG, 107.

[140] Grk *koluo*, GT, 366 & AG, 461.

[141] Grk *ekballo* here "expel someone from a group, repudiate someone" (AG, 237; cf. GT, 192f). Compare the use in John 9:34f.

[142] Grk preposition *ek*, out of. He derives from God. He has been begotten of God, and God is his Father.

Plainly John is describing Diotrephes as a doer of evil not to be imitated by Gaius. It may be true, as some hold, that Diotrephes was not sympathetic to the false teaching combated in Second John. Perhaps he saw John and the men sent from him as threats to his own position, and he cared for nothing but the preserving of his own position. But whatever his motives, the man had refused support to the teachers of the truth and placed himself in the company of evil doers who had no experience of God, in fact the same company as the false teachers (cf. 2 John 11). By not showing love to the brothers, by breaking fellowship with them and with the apostles, he had also placed himself outside the fellowship with God (cf. 1 John 1:1–4).

Diotrephes was not to be imitated. But another man, Demetrius, was coming to Gaius with impeccable credentials, and John gives his endorsement to this man in verse 12. Demetrius may have been the bearer of the letter, one of the traveling evangelists, or both. Demetrius, says John, has three witnesses to his good character: (a) He has the witness of all, evidently meaning all the brothers who know him. (b) He has the testimony of the truth itself. As one who like Gaius himself (cf. 3) walked in the truth, the truth itself was a witness to his character. (c) Finally, "we [emphatic in Greek] also bear witness, and you know that our witness is true." The plural probably refers to John and his fellow witnesses (cf. 1 John 1:1–4). Notice that this is a third witness, added to "the witness of all," so that it has to be explained with reference to a special group.

Conclusion (13–15)

The third epistle closes as did the second. "I had many things to write to you," John writes, phrasing his words from the standpoint of the reader as he reads the letter, "but I do not wish to write to you with ink and pen" (13). The Greek *kalamos* means a reed and here refers to a reed pen (AG, 398; cf. GT, 321). *With ink and pen* takes the place of *with paper and ink* in the second epistle (12), but the meaning is the same in effect. John continues: "But I hope to see you right away[143] and we will talk mouth to mouth," as in Second John 12. The Elder closes with a wish for peace, sends greetings from "the friends" where

---

[143] Grk *eutheos*, GT, 258 & AG, 320.

he is and requests that greetings be given to "the friends" where Gaius is "by name," which probably means individually.   Diotrephes loved position and status (Grk *philoproteuo*), and was not friendly toward those who came bearing the truth.   *The friends* were those "loved ones"[144] in every place who were bonded together by common loyalty to the truth (2 John 1–3; 2 John 1–4, 8).

---

[144] Grk *philoi*, nominative plural of *philos*. See GT, 654 & AG, 861.

Order Books & Tapes by L. A. Mott, Jr.

Telephone: 904/268-2667

E-mail: service@sunesispublishing.com

Postal Mail: Sunesis Publishing Company, 11908 Gran Meadows Way,
Jacksonville, FL 32258

To order by mail, clip this order form, write in the blanks the quantity of each item you wish to order, figure the total on the back, fill in your address at the bottom, and send to the postal address above. Your satisfaction is always guaranteed.

Thinking Through the Bible Series

A set of study guides filled with thought-provoking questions and insightful exposition aimed at guiding the diligent student through the thought processes of the Bible's writers (Books on Philippians and John's Epistles are exposition only, without questions). Cassette recordings of class lectures are also available. The books have perfect binding (*Philippians*), a comb binding (c), or a special "lay-flat" binding called *Otabind* (O).

___ *Wisdom and Poetry* (88 pp., c) $7.95
    ___ Lessons on Cassette $50
___ *John* (160 pp., comb) $11.95
    ___ Lessons on Cassette $50
___ *Acts* (119 pp., comb) $9.95
    ___ Lessons on Cassette $45
___ *Romans* (51 pp., comb) $6.50
    ___ Lessons on Cassette $25
___ *Second Corinthians*
(126 pp., Otabind) $11.95
    ___ Lessons on Cassette $25

___ *Philippians* (123 pp.) $8.95
    ___ Lessons on Cassette $25
    (includes Eph. & Col.)
___ *Hebrews & James* (56 pp., c) $6.50
    ___ Lessons on Cassette $25
___ *John's Epistles* (124 pp., O) $11.95
    ___ 1 Pe.–Jude on Cassette $25
___ *Revelation* (123 pp., O) $11.95
    ___ Lessons on Cassette $25

___ **Entire series to date**—$65.75

Booklets *($2 each or > 10 copies @ $1 each)*
___ *Instrumental Music in Worship: A Biblical/Historical Approach*
___ *Keeping Saved: God's Good Gifts to Preserve His People*

Name _____

Address _____

City_____ State_____ Zip _____

Telephone _____

E-Mail _____

All prices subject to change without notice.
For more information, contact Sunesis Publishing or see www.sunesispublishing.com

Study Guides and Tape Recorded Courses on the Books of the Bible

___ Genesis $3.00

   ___ *Lessons on Cassette* ($25)

___ Exodus & Leviticus $4.00

   ___ *Lessons on Cassette* ($25)

___ Numbers/Deuteronomy $2.80

   ___ *Lessons on Cassette* ($25)

___ Joshua–Ruth $1.50

   ___ *Lessons on Cassette* ($25)

___ United Kingdom $5.00

   ___ *Lessons on Cassette* ($50)

___ Divided Kingdom $1.60

   ___ *Lessons on Cassette* ($25)

___ Preexilic Minor Prophets $1.60

   ___ *Lessons on Cassette* ($25)

___ Exile and Return $2.25

   ___ *Lessons on Cassette* ($50)

___ Matthew *(tape set only)* $50

___ Mark $1.25

   ___ *Lessons on Cassette* ($25)

___ Luke $1.75

   ___ *Lessons on Cassette* ($50)

___ First Cor. $3.00

   ___ *Lessons on Cassette* ($25)

___ Second Cor./Gal. $2.00

   ___ *Lessons on Cassette* ($25)

___ Eph.–Col. $1.25

   ___ *Lessons on Cassette* ($25)

___ First Thess.—Philemon $2.95

   ___ *Lessons on Cassette* ($25)

___ First Peter–Jude $3.00

   ___ *Lessons on Cassette* ($25)

___ All 15 Study Guides ($27.75)

Monographs on Vital Bible Themes (8-16 pages each)

One free; a dozen for $7.50; 25–99, 50 cents each; 100 for $35. One of each, $10.

___   1. The Resurrection of Jesus Christ (the evidence of John)
___   2. The First Day Meeting at Troas (Acts 20:7 and the Lord's supper)
___   3. Reading Revelation (basic approach to the book of Revelation)
___   4. Song of Solomon (complete analysis)
___   5. Redemption in Christ Jesus (death of Christ: table talks on Romans)
___   6. The Sinner's Prayer: Calling on the Name of the Lord
___   7. Wives and Husbands (exposition of Ephesians 5:22–33)
___   8. Paul Before Agrippa: The Case for Christianity
___   9. Which Thief on the Cross? (answer to rebuttal on baptism)
___   10. The Good News for Business People (Conversion of Lydia)
___   11. Glorying in the Cross (death of Christ: table talks from Galatians)
___   12. The Great Commission (complete analysis of Matthew 28:18–20)
       13. Birth From Above (discussion of John 3:5 in context)
___   14. The Deity of Jesus Christ (emphasis on John 1:1-3)
___   15. The Ministry of Reconciliation (exposition of 2 Cor. 5:11–6:2)
___   16. Messiah on Trial (the temptation of Jesus)
___   17. The Collection for the Saints (exposition of 2 Cor. 8 & 9)
___   18. Baptism, Grace and Justification (Romans)
___   19. Christians at War (exposition of Ephesians 6:10–20)
___   20. The Apostolic Office in the New Testament
___   21. Righteousness as a Distinguishing Mark of the Children of God (exposition of First John 2:28–3:12, from *Thinking Through John's Epistles*)

Total Price_____ + 10% s/h _____ + 6% tax _____ =

                      minimum of $3.50   Florida Residents Only

Total of Order _____   (monographs min. $1)